SEDUCTION OF BLACK CRIMINALITY

To Shurry,
your support means
the world to me!
Be blessed,
Gm 2009

GENE A. JONES

CGS COMMUNICATIONS
FORT WORTH, TEXAS

The Seduction of Black Criminality
Copyright ©1996
by Gene A. Jones

CGS Communications
Publishing Company
Post Office Box 17485
Fort Worth, Texas 76102

First printing May 1996

Library of Congress Catalog Card Number 96-85172

Publisher's Cataloging in Publication
(Prepared by Quality Books, Inc.)

Jones, Gene A.
  The seduction of Black criminality : a psychopolitical analysis of Black crime in America / Gene A. Jones.
  p. cm.
  Includes bibliographical references and index.
  ISBN 0-9650505-0-5

  1. Crime--United States. 2. Afro-Americans--Social conditions. 3. Racism--United States. 4. United States--Race relations. 5. Afro-American criminals. I. Title.

HV6488.J66 1996   364'.089'960973
                                            QBI9620322

Cover design by Larry Powell & Associates

Printed in the United States of America.

DISCLAIMER

DEDICATION

Dedicated to the memory of my beloved grandmother, Katie Mae Boyd, who passed before this book was published. To my precious little girl, Ashley—Daddy loves ya! And a special dedication to the memory of my intellectual hero, Dr. Amos N. Wilson, whose writings inspired me to write this book, and who kindly set aside many hours of his personal time to talk with me regarding this project.

TABLE OF CONTENTS

ACKNOWLEDGMENTS

I extend my deepest gratitude and sincere appreciation to my mom, Daisy Jones, for her love and unwavering support. To Scheretta Scott for lending me her time to read, proof and assist in research, for needed encouragement, and for utilizing her computer skills to make this a quality piece of literature. To Pamela Dunlop-Gates for her direction, patience and willingness to assist me with this project, particularly when it was in its rough stages. To Dr. Cornel Thomas for his encouragement, proofing and counsel.

To Dr. Brenda Wall for providing feedback and the foreword. To Renee Harris and Joyce Ann Brown for their commentary. To Bob Ray Sanders, Sababu Plata, Reverend Roosevelt Sutton, Dr. Chinita Heard, Detective Michael Carroll and Sergeant Naymond James for their critiques. To Dr. Robert Bing III, Dr. Bernard Headley, Sergeant Janice Willingham and Ella Collins-Nelson for providing me with valuable pieces of information.

To all the authors I quoted in this book and whose work provided a basis for the formulation of some of my ideas. To the staff at the Fort Worth Public Library East Berry and Central branches for always providing me with courteous and helpful service. To everyone who encouraged me to continue writing when the community newsletter I produced entitled *Polytechnic Heights Good In The Hood* was no longer being published. To Carolyn Bullard who edited the manuscript as though it were her own. And to my publisher for opening a door of opportunity for a young brother.

Foreword

As we approach the beginning of the next millennium, the African American community continues to face unrelenting, destructive social pressures. These often immobilizing pressures are manifest in the well-known statistics pertaining to teen pregnancy, substance abuse, high school dropouts, AIDS, unemployment, poverty, gang violence, and crime. The African American community is plagued by disturbingly high occurrences of practically any social phenomenon that has as its outcome the devastation of African identity, family and community stability.

A notable exception is its development and nurturing of the institutional Black church. This relates to the co-existing positive dynamic within the African American community, which demonstrates a powerful momentum to resist oppressive forces and often overcome seemingly impossible conditions. These victories are evident in the record numbers of African Americans in political, corporate, academic and entrepreneurial offices. While these achievements are significant, the most important victory is clearly the presence of African American thinkers and activists who embrace liberation as a goal. Without this critical remnant, many would be unable to interpret just how the dynamics of racism and oppression are related to the statistics of despair as well as to the celebrated accomplishments of a few—a few who almost always lack the consciousness that would make them most useful to a community under social siege.

Without this remnant, there would be no meaningful understanding of how the socially appropriate debates on affirmative action, welfare reform, and crime mask the socially unacceptable acts of repression that make the rich richer and the exploited more confused and vulnerable. Without this remnant, there would be no commitment to freedom that would lead children away from hopelessness, adolescents away from gangs, men away from prisons, and families away from disintegration.

The late Dr. Amos Wilson represented this remnant in a most noble way. He dedicated his life to generating information to serve as a North Star to our freedom. His analysis, inspiration and service are evident in his scholarly books, in his taped lectures, and in the many lives he touched. The author of this timely volume, Gene Jones, represents one whose life and work was touched by Dr. Wilson. Gene has courageously accepted the torch passed to him by Dr. Wilson, and in this introductory work, exhibits a profound understanding of the complexity of African American life. His psychopolitical analysis of Black crime is powerful. It leaves the reader feeling that the possibility for liberation and social responsibility is as close at hand as the demoralizing images of the criminalized Black man on the evening news.

We are very fortunate that a police officer from Fort Worth, Texas has accepted the call for freedom, which is reflected in his local community work and in his determination to share a perspective which is hidden from the American public. His inspired commitment shines forth in this volume. In *The Seduction of Black Criminality*, there is the much needed analysis of crime as it is inextricably interwoven in the dynamics of racism and African American oppression. He takes the analysis a step further by forcing each of us to examine how we must accept personal responsibility for securing safety and empowerment. He gives answers.

As we anticipate the rise in the prison industry as the "new slave trade" for the turn of the millennium, it is vital that we understand how these profits from warehousing human lives will be accumulated. We must understand just how African men and women are being programmed to become the victims of the ongoing racist oppression through criminalization and fear tactics. The ruling elite is eager in their greed and in their politics of conservative revolution. However, with strong, new voices such as Gene Jones', there is the opportunity to upset the evil forces of aggression and racism, and to usher in an era of justice and peace.

It is a blessing and an honor to contribute the foreword for this historic text. Gene has been a warrior for peace in Fort Worth, and illustrates the power which comes from being in the establishment system of oppression, but not of the establishment mind set. As you read, may you be united with the many voices of freedom, which he so brilliantly represents, and may you also be inspired to join in the struggle for peace and justice.

Brenda Wall, Ph.D.
Juneteenth, 1995

INTRODUCTION

This book is about three operations that are traceable throughout American history. The first is the operation of criminalizing Blacks through criminal justice involvement, and their "seduction into criminality" with oppressive treatment. The second is the operation of criminalizing the image of Black people. And the final operation involves using Black people's criminalized image and exaggerated acts of crime and violence to justify their exploitation and abuse by the American social system.

My observations of inner-city neighborhoods in Milwaukee, Wisconsin and Fort Worth, Texas, the criminal justice system at large, varied experiences as a police officer, and a book entitled *Black-on-Black Violence* by the late Dr. Amos Wilson, provided a window that permitted me to identify these operations, which I named The Seduction of Black Criminality. This process will also be referred to as the seduction machination throughout this book.

The first seven essays are devoted to unraveling this process, and the final essay examines how it can be terminated. The first essay entitled, *Lies and Half Truths about Crime in the Black Community*, identifies the "culprits of misinformation." These culprits mislead the nation about Black crime and non-Black crime in America. The whole notion that America's crime and drug problems are **"Black"** is generated by these culprits. They blindfold the eyes of many Americans, preventing them from realizing how deeply crime and violence penetrate the soil the entire nation.

White Domination, Black Criminality discusses the relationship between White domination and Black crime. It unveils the fundamental function of the ensemble of Black crime, criminalized Black images, and the myths of Black crime in the American social system. This essay reveals the historical use of the mass media with regard to White American perception. And it sheds the light of understanding on the question of why a measurable number of Black males in America are socially, economically and politically weakened.

Oppressive Strategies that Seduce Blacks into Crime discusses the three types of violence Whites inflicted on African Americans and examines how these degrading experiences ushered African Americans into a cycle of self-degradation. This understanding is vital to the neutralization of crime in the Black community. It helps African Americans understand their problems so that they can prescribe meaningful remedies for healing and restoration.

Post-Segregation Black Parents: Unwitting Agents of the Seduction? is a bold analysis of the effects of the "Black experience" in America and the decade of the '70s on Black parenthood. These two unique experiences produced two types of Black parents who unwittingly participate in the seduction machination. This essay emphasizes that in order for Blacks in America to ensure their existence they must see to it that their children achieve optimal intellectual and emotional development.

The Psychology of Gangsterism: It Existed Long Before Monster Kody deals with the mind of the violent Black criminal. It responds to the often asked question: "Why do Blacks commit Black-on-Black violence." This essay also discusses America's obsession with the violent Black criminal. Mainstream media portray the violent Black criminal as a peculiar "monster." However, America fails to understand that when it looks at the violent Black criminal on the evening news it sees its own likeness.

Seduced by the Legal Institution: Chronicling Attacks on Black People by America's Legal System explores the historical over-arching purpose of the justice system in the African American community. It reveals how the ruling elite have intentionally misused laws and law enforcers to crush Black organization, maintain social dominance and acquire tremendous wealth.

Justice or Justified Oppression? discusses the related concepts of "justified oppression" and "institutional criminalization." It discusses how the very structure of American culture breeds two brands of justice — "White Justice," and "Black Justice." This essay discusses how members of the justice system can abuse Blacks without some considering it abuse, and how Blacks can be treated unfairly in the courts without some considering it injustice.

Countering the Seduction supplies viable solutions to eradicating the seduction machination. It offers a 13-point framework involving reactive and proactive measures. This essay challenges the efficacy of White liberal and moderate philosophy regarding eradicating Black crime. And it explains that if the African American community fails to take responsibility for terminating this demeaning process, it could likely terminate them.

Though the term machination, which means a plot, conspiracy or scheme, is used to characterize this process, the reader should not presume that it is composed solely of individuals and groups who consciously discriminate against, abuse and induce Blacks into crime and violence. Many individuals and groups unconsciously participate in this process. Blacks have been treated as inferiors for such a long time in America that it seems normal to some. Others work in organizations that are sustained politically and/or economically through the discrimination, abuse and inducement of Blacks into crime. However, there are those who intentionally engage in some of these activities for economic and political reasons.

I trust the provocative nature of this book will cause you to take a more objective and critical look at the whole matter of Black crime. Moreover, I trust it will raise the level of discussion and open up more meaningful doors of dialogue amongst all people concerning this and related matters. Above all, I hope this book enlightens and inspires Black readers, and others genuinely interested in the liberation of Black people, to press forward through God's grace toward that high goal.

Gene A. Jones
Fort Worth, Texas
1996

ONE

LIES AND HALF TRUTHS ABOUT CRIME IN THE BLACK COMMUNITY

The subject of Black crime is covered with a blanket woven from myths and false images. Pulling the blanket off this subject is vitally necessary to the eradication of crime and violence in the Black community. The common American perception of Black communities, particularly urban, is they are overrun with rapists, robbers, drug addicts, drug dealers, murderers and other criminals. Why do Americans tend to think crime and violence are far more egregious and rampant in Black communities?

No one is surprised when crack is confiscated from the "projects" in South Central Los Angeles or the west side of Chicago. However, many people are shocked when heroin and cocaine are hauled out of middle-class suburban houses in Dallas or St. Louis. When Blacks pull car-jackings and rob convenience stores in the ghetto, it is deemed normal to Black ghetto culture. However, when White corporate executives embezzle millions of dollars from savings and loan institutions, it is looked at as an aberration. It must be understood that crime and violence are not monopolized by Blacks. They are American traditions.

Polls conducted throughout 1994 consistently revealed that crime and violence weighed heaviest on the American mind. The Bureau of Justice Statistics (1994) reports that in February 1974, 29 percent of the American population was concerned most about unemployment, while 4 percent were

1

concerned most about crime. However, in January 1994, 18 percent were concerned most about unemployment, while 37 percent were concerned most about crime. Notice that crime and violence surpassed money matters to become the nation's foremost domestic concern. The message contained in this shift of domestic priorities is that Americans had become more concerned about how they were going to live to see the next day than how they were going to make a living day-to-day.

Many African Americans believe the myths of the "crime-ridden Black community" and the "law-abiding White suburb." African Americans who accept these lies as truth must realize that their acceptance gives credence to absurd rationales put forth by Whites to legitimize their mistreatment of African Americans. It is in the interest of African Americans to be committed to stripping bare every lie and false image projected about the African American community. Some African American institutions participate in the gross process of promoting lies and projecting negative images of Black people. Black magazines print tragic stories that illustrate the horror of "Black-on-Black" violence. Gangsta rappers beat out poignant lyrics in their songs and project criminalized images in their videos that smear Blacks with crime. Their intentions may be noble, but unfortunately they portray urban Black communities as places spilling over with gun-toting males, drug dealers, thieves, robbers, etc.

People who accept lies and false images of Black crime without question are co-contributors to the psychological conspiracy that generates a negative perception of Blacks and self-hate within their consciousness. The actual seriousness of crime and violence in the African American community, and the veritable threat they pose to their survivability are clearly irrefutable. The social phenomenon labeled "Black-on-Black" violence has become another piece among the arsenal of weaponry used in the "Black genocide." In segregated America, the White supremacy system waged the most vicious assault on African Americans, bar none. However, in post-segregation America the social phenomenon of "Black-on-Black" violence has emerged and has landed lethal blows to many African Americans.

The collapse of Jim Crow/legal segregation did not devastate the White supremacy system. It merely transformed its means of expression and methods of operation. White supremacy was no longer covertly operable. It became functional through the operational policies and laws of institutions.

The deadly dynamic of intra-racial violence, which a measurable minority of Blacks participate in, works in concert with institutional White supremacy to wreak havoc on the African American community. Observe these alarming statistics regarding intra-racial crime and violence in the African American community, and their consequences.

- During 1979 to 1986 the violent crime victimization rate for persons age 12 or older was 44 per 1,000 blacks, and 34 per 1,000 whites. Blacks experienced higher rates of rape, robbery, and aggravated assault, but whites had higher rates of simple assault and personal theft.
- Blacks had higher robbery rates than whites for both males and females. Robbery rates per 1,000 persons were 18 robberies for black males, 7 for white males, 9 for black females, and 4 for white females.
- In central cities, blacks had higher robbery and household burglary rates than whites, regardless of the age or family income of the victim or household head.
- In aggravated assaults, black victims were more likely than white victims to be injured. Black victims injured in violent crimes were more likely to sustain serious injuries than white victims. **Source: Bureau of Justice Statistics, *Black Victims*, 1990.**

- Except for crimes of theft and simple assault, blacks were significantly more likely than whites or persons of other races, such as Asians or Native Americans, to be victims of crime. For instance, in 1992 there were 15.6 robberies for every 1,000 black persons, 4.7 for every 1,000 whites, and 5.1 for every 1,000 persons in other racial categories. **Source: Bureau of Justice Statistics, *Criminal Victimization*, 1992.**

- In 1992, black males 12 to 24 years of age experienced violent crime at a rate significantly higher than the rates for other age or racial groups. Males 16 to 19 years of age were particularly at risk; their violent victimization rate was almost double the rate for white males and three times that for white females in the same age range.
- While black males 16 and 24 years of age comprised only about 1 percent of the population age 12 or over in 1992, they experienced 5 percent of all violent victimization. **Source: Bureau of Justice Statistics, *Young Black Male Victims*, 1994.**

- Homicide is the leading cause of death for black males 15 to 24 years of age.
- The homicide rate among black men 15 to 24 years of age rose by 66 percent from 1984 to 1987.
- For black males 15 to 19 years of age, firearm homicides have increased 125 percent since 1984. **Source: Crime in the United States, *Federal Bureau of Investigation Uniform Crime Report*, 1988.**

- In 1993, 94 percent of blacks killed were slain by black offenders.
- In 1993, blacks comprised approximately 12 percent of the United States population. Yet, during that year blacks accounted for 31 percent of all arrests reported to the FBI. **Source: Crime in the United States,** *Federal Bureau of Investigation Uniform Crime Reports,* **1993.**

- Of the persons arrested for murder in 1992, blacks accounted for 55.1 percent of the total. That same year, blacks accounted for 42.8 percent of all arrests for rape, 60.9 percent of all arrests for robbery, 38.8 percent for aggravated assault, 30.4 percent for burglary, 31.4 percent for larceny/theft, and 39.4 percent for auto theft.
- From 1987 to 1992, 39.7 percent of black males 16 to 19 years of age have been victims of handgun crimes. **Source:** *Statistical Abstract of the United States,* **1994.**

- An estimated 32.2 percent, or 827,440 black men in their 20s are being supervised by the criminal justice system. **Source: Bureau of Justice Statistics,** *Young Black Americans and the Criminal Justice System: Five Years Later,* **1995.**

- On March 1, 1987, there were a total of 1,874 prisoners under sentence of death. Of that number, 777 or 42 percent were black. **Source: National Urban League State of Black America 1988,** *Crime in the Black Community.*

- Sixty-five percent of prison inmates belonged to racial or ethnic minorities in 1991, up from 60 percent in 1986.

	1986	1991
White	40%	35%
Black	45%	46%

Source: *Bureau of Justice Statistics Survey of State Prison Inmates,* **1991.**

- In 1992 there were 195,156 blacks incarcerated in jails in the United States; in 1991 there were 336,920 blacks incarcerated in stateprisons. **Source:** *Statistical Abstract of the United States,* **1994.**

Crime Statistics Fail to Tell the Whole Truth about Crime in America

Many crime reports and related statistical sources arouse legitimate concerns and irrational fears over crime and violence in the African American community. They generate White hysteria and cause Americans, and the world, to peg Black Americans, particularly young Black males, as a "class of criminals."

Many statistics are classic examples of the adage that looks are deceiving. Conclusive judgments about Blacks based strictly on crime reports are likely to be incorrect. It cannot be refuted that crime and violence in the African American community are at critical levels. However, what is refutable is the usability of crime reports as definitive sources of accurate crime measurement in the United States. Most crime reports portray Black crime as the most menacing and threatening kind in America's subculture of crime. Statistics such as those previously cited serve as part of the philosophical foundation by which false notions are constructed in the American mind regarding Black crime and Black people in America.

Crime reports contribute to the opinion embraced by many African Americans, particularly the detached bourgeoisie, that racism/White supremacy is not one of the African American community's greatest impediments. Crime reports support their opinion that the collection of criminal and violent Blacks are the Black community's greatest impediment.

These deceptive numbers are also a major piece of the philosophical foundation that supports the notion that Blacks are genetically predisposed to crime and violence. This devilish notion is currently being promoted by a band of pop-scientists, philosophers and other people in health professions such as Charles Murray, co-author of the controversial book *The Bell Curve*.

These misleading statistics contaminate attitudes, falsify perceptions, and confuse the understanding of many Americans of crime and violence in the United States. They prevent many African Americans from fully realizing the harsh reality of racism/White supremacy and its multiple adverse effects on contemporary Black America. These individuals tend to focus critically on "Black-on-Black" violence while discounting, or ignoring, the pain and lethal affects of racism/White supremacy in the collective African American community. This neglect empowers racism/White supremacy, enabling it to better thwart the development and progress of the collective African American community.

The Negative Effects of Labeling Black Crime

In the late '60s, intra-racial crime in the Black community was given the dubious label "Black-on-Black" crime. This term has been used quite generously in press reports, criminological studies and casual conversations of people throughout the country. The effects of the generous usage of the term "Black-on-Black" crime and violence have been adverse and can be seen within every level of African American life and personality, i.e., psychological, political, social and economical.

How ironic it is that while most victims of crime and violence in America are victimized by someone of their race, crime and violence in the Black community are singled out and labeled "Black-on-Black." Why aren't the terms "White-on-White," "Asian-on-Asian" and "Hispanic-on-Hispanic" used as generously as "Black-on-Black" crime? The dubious labeling of crime and violence in the Black community as "Black-on-Black" embitters White attitudes and distorts their perception of Blacks. Most importantly, this label contaminates the attitudes and perceptions Blacks hold of themselves.

People generally do not fully appreciate the power and effect labels can have on attitude, perception and thought. The labeling of crime in the Black community as "Black-on-Black" functions as a psychological virus infecting public perception of all Blacks. The label "Black-on-Black" suggests three things. First, that Blacks are their single greatest nemesis. Second, that Black criminals are subhuman and animalistic. Third, that Black crime is more deplorable than crime in other racial categories.

This negative label also plucks Black criminality from the historical and social roots from which it stems. This prevents students and researchers of Black crime from realizing its core causes. The term "Black-on-Black" suggests that Black people and Black sociology are the primary—or exclusive—sources of the Black community's crime problem. The focus on Black sociology discounts long-term Black oppression as a source.

Startling crime and arrest statistics about Black criminality, mass media's criminalization of the Black image, and the abundant usage of the negative term "Black-on-Black" crime and violence provide fertile soil for the sprouting notion that the problem of Black crime is the product of a criminal class. The ruling elite uses this idea to advance their goals. With coded phraseology, they state that it is a waste to invest in a criminal class. Consequently, the nation's governmental leadership seems justified in rolling back the gains of African Americans and programs that protect them from the tyranny of the majority. Whites also use the "criminal class" notion to discredit those who assert that Black oppression is a huge contributor to many Black problems, particularly Black crime and violence.

MYTH PERPETUATION LEADS TO HUMAN DEVASTATION

The ruling elite project and promote lies, and truth mixed with lies, about African Americans. Their primary mode of promotion and projection is the media. Lies and half truths that are specific to a certain race can also be called racial myths. For purposes of this book, the term racial myth is defined as:

notions drawn that are based upon erroneous scientific studies, inaccurate statistical data, lies, falsified imagery and other unreliable sources that are aimed at a certain race.

Racial myths are psychosocial mechanisms one group uses to maintain dominance over another group. Myths should not be viewed as mere pieces of inconsequential false information. They are tremendously potent instruments of perceptual, attitudinal and conceptual manipulation. Myths, though false, are considered by many to be truly accurate and correct pieces of information.

The consequences of racial myths on their intended targets can range from mildly inconvenient situations to deadly outcomes. One of the most dramatic and tragic demonstrations of racial myths having deadly consequences upon a targeted group is the extermination of more than 1.5 million Native Americans by Europeans between 1492 and 1890. The rationale behind this oppressive treatment were the myths that Europeans were inherently superior and Native Americans were "savages." These myths legitimized the capture and slaughter of hundreds of thousands of Native American men, women, boys and girls.

Comedian Jackie Mason may or may not be aware that racial myths contain tremendous psychic power and can infect the human psyche. On *Pat Buchanan and Company*, Mason commented:

> The black people are more susceptible to violence in this country than any other denomination . . . By far the majority of any kind of violence that's taking place in this country, happens to be coming from the black community . . . One out of four black youths will eventually wind up in jail. What percentage of white people wind up in jail[1]?

Mason does not monopolize the industry of racial mythification. These views are embraced by many Americans. His thoughts, and those similar, are shaped and molded by myths and misinformation about Black crime, and Blacks in general. Myths were often created and projected by Whites for the purpose of legitimizing Black oppression and White dominance over America's political and economic systems. This holds true in contemporary American society as well. I wish to dispel what I believe are three of the most common and dangerous myths that exist today regarding Black criminality and crime in the Black community.

MYTH #1
BLACKS ARE MORE PRONE TO CRIME AND VIOLENCE THAN WHITES

In the latter 1800s, certain scientists in America and Europe engaged in a conspiracy of slander. They published articles in various scientific journals, wrote books and conducted studies that denigrated the Black personality. Many asserted that Black people were biologically predisposed to crime and violence. A German doctor named Frank Hoffman condemned Black males, declaring that there was such an "immense amount of immorality and crime" among them. He attributed this to their "race traits and tendencies." Charles Carroll, author of the book entitled *The Negro a Beast or in the Image of God*, published in 1900 by the American Book and Bible House, likewise assailed the character and personality of Black people. He referred to them as "dangerous," of "massive size," and "threatening."

History has gone full circle. The attack on Black character and personality by the scientific establishment has developed alarming strength over the last decade. Conferences are held by reputable colleges throughout the country where the notions of inherent Black intellectual inferiority and a link between Black crime and Black genes are serious topics of discussion. Pop-science is not the only tool being used to construct the myth of Black proneness to crime and violence. Official statistical sources relative to crime and violence, and the typecasting of African Americans as ultra-criminal and super-aggressive in mass media are other tools being used. The most common statistical sources relative to crime and violence are arrest and incarceration reports. These sources, coupled with criminalized Black images burned in the nation's mind by mass media, makes to many people the absurd notion that Black people possess a criminal personality or are prone to crime and violence seem worth considering. These sources will be examined in the order in which they were mentioned.

CRIME/ARREST REPORTS

The Federal Bureau of Investigation Uniform Crime Report (UCR) is regarded by many law enforcement professionals as the "Bible" of crime and arrest reports in America. However, this document is not a dependable instrument for precise crime measurement. The UCR is the product of local, state and federal crime and arrest reports compiled and compared against U.S. Census Bureau figures. Consequently, inaccuracies in these reports will be reflected in the UCR. Why are the UCR and other crime and arrest reports inaccurate? I will offer eight contributing factors.

1. EXPUNCTION OF CRIMINAL RECORDS

The ability to have criminal records expunged—deleted from the records system—contributes significantly to the disproportionate number of Black arrests shown on many crime/arrest reports. The District Clerk's Office of Tarrant County, Texas reported that during the period of September 1993 to September 1994 a total of 88 expunction cases were disposed. The District Clerk's Office only maintains the actual number of expunction cases filed and disposed.

As a result, the racial breakdown of expunction cases is unknown.However, my conversations with police detectives, attorneys and judges reveal that White Americans clearly make more petitions for expunction than African Americans, and are granted more expunctions than African Americans as well. I am aware of only one African American who has had their criminal record expunged. It is safe to presume that statistics for White arrests are measurably decreased because of the greater number of expunctions they receive.

2. RACE AND ECONOMICS

The psychology of making arrests is affected by certain variables. The way these variables impact an officer's decision-making capacity, in terms of making arrests, decreases the number of legally attainable White arrests. Probably the two most common variables are the racial and socioeconomic status of victims and offenders. For instance, officers are likely to walk into a domestic disturbance situation in a middle- or upper middle-class White residential neighborhood and offer the disputing individuals tempered advice or counseling. However, in poor Black neighborhoods, it is not unusual to see one or both disputing parties issued citations or transported to jail.

Death penalty statistics reveal that the racial status of murderers and their victims affect the psychology of judges and juries. The chances of a murderer being sentenced to death for killing a White person are ten times greater than for killing a Black person[2].

3. ERRORS IN TITLING REPORTS

Officers sometimes title criminal offense reports incorrectly. This error manifests with disproportionate numbers of Black arrests. This often occurs with violent offenses, particularly aggravated assaults. For instance, when an assault suspect is Black, officers are more apt to upgrade the offense to an aggravated classification. Studies underscore this observation. In the July 1993 issue of *Social Work* magazine, Dr. Evan Stark wrote:

> Overresponse by police characterizes the treatment of black teenagers. When white and black teenagers commit the same offense, police are seven times more likely to charge black teenagers with a felony.

The overcharging of Black suspects by officers with respects to certain violent offenses makes it appear on some crime reports as though Blacks are far more violent than other groups.

4. REPEAT ARRESTEES

A significant number of individuals arrested in the African American communities throughout this nation are repeat arrestees. Individuals in the African American community who sell and use drugs, prostitute, abuse family members and commit other crimes are largely a certain group of people who are repeatedly arrested for these offenses. The vast majority of people in the African American community are law-abiding people. Most crime reports give the impression that each arrest tallied in its report is a separate incident committed by a different individual. Many do not clearly inform the reader that many of these offenses are committed by repeat offenders.

5. EASY ACCESS TO WEAPONS/RECKLESSNESS

The proliferation and easy availability of firearms contributes to the alarming numbers of homicides and related arrests of Blacks that appear on the UCR. The escalating use of hand guns and assault weapons contributes to the high numbers of victims of violent incidents in the Black community. The spraying of bullets in the infamous drive-by shooting often leaves the intended target or targets, as well as unintended individuals, injured or fatally wounded. Deaths that occurred due to recklessness can be classified as homicides in some reports opposed to unintentional homicides. It is highly likely that the actual number of *intentional* homicides in the Black community is lower than what is reflected on the UCR.

6. MORE AGGRESSIVE POLICING IN BLACK NEIGHBORHOODS

Law enforcement agencies tend to employ their most aggressive enforcement tactics most frequently in Black communities. White communities see fewer "zero tolerance strategies," "street sweeps," and other similar operations than the Black community. Therefore, the number of White arrests is much lower than the number of crimes they actually commit. Blacks, however, are poured into the justice system through street sweeps and other aggressive operations.

7. THE DISADVANTAGE OF LESS MONEY AND CONNECTIONS

Whites have a larger "safety net" than Blacks. Whites have more money and inside connections to the justice system at their disposal than Blacks. While the actual number of White arrests is higher than Blacks, these resources assist in their being aborted from the criminal justice process in greater numbers than Blacks. Blacks however have the disadvantage of less money and connections and therefore are unable to escape processing as often as Whites. This disparity widens the gap between Black arrests and White arrests.

8. UNDETECTED CRIMES

This factor probably contributes to the unreliability of crime and arrest reports more than the first seven combined. Knowledgeable law enforcement professionals are aware that a great deal of crime in America goes undetected and unreported. In *Community Policing,* Robert Trojanowicz and Bonnie Bucqueroux underscore this by writing:

> The answers to how much crime exists in the United States are simple—no one knows. At best, indicators such as the Uniform Crime Reporting (UCR) statistics compiled by the FBI show trends, but they do not provide a true picture of the number of crimes actually committed at any specific time. As the National Crime Survey verifies, most crimes are never reported to the police. According to the *Report to the Nation on Crime and Justice—Second Edition,* only about one-third of all crimes are reported. Even when police are notified, changes in reporting procedures and complications within the system make it likely that many crimes are omitted from national totals.

The type of crimes that are most unaccounted for in America are crimes committed by white-collar criminals, a.k.a. "suite-criminals." White-collar offenses include embezzlement, fraud, tax evasion, bribery, kickbacks and business violations. The criminal justice system tends to be kinder to white-collar criminals. White-collar criminals can obtain the best attorneys money can buy, and these attorneys are well connected to the power brokers of the political and judicial systems in America. Consequently, they are able to manipulate the system to the benefit of their client. Political interests cause some judges to display soft attitudes toward white-collar criminals.

White-collar trials are generally lengthy. This gives attorneys greater opportunity to find errors during trial and obtain a mistrial. Witnesses often back out of white-collar trials because they become exasperated by the long waiting period between indictment and the end of the trial. And if white-collar criminals are convicted and sentenced to prison, they pay their debt to society in environments that are more comfortable than those of many hard-working citizens.

Furthermore, white-collar criminals are often able to maintain a large portion of their criminal spoil because the fines imposed upon them are often far less than the money they stole.

Due to these factors, crime/arrest reports do not accurately reflect the state of crime in Black America or in America at large. Crime in every demographic section of America could easily be two or three times higher than what the UCR reflects, especially crime in the White community. Crime/ arrest reports actually say more about economic disparity, racial bias, discrimination and institutional racism in the law enforcement and judicial systems than the actual state of crime in the United States.

PRISON STATISTICS

Prison statistics are another undependable instrument to measure crime in America. They too are more indicative of economic disparity, racial bias, discrimination and institutional racism within the judicial system than crime in America. Study and research of the judicial process (courts) have solidly proved that it sends Blacks to prison more frequently and for longer periods of time than Whites. Numerous studies reveal the chilling fact that third-time White offenders are consistently given shorter sentences than first-time African American offenders who committed the same crime. This matter is looked into in greater depth in chapter seven, *Justice or Justified Oppression?*

PRINT AND ELECTRONIC NEWS MEDIA

The November 12, 1990 copy of *Jet* magazine contained a story dealing with a study conducted by The Center for Media and Public Affairs in Washington, D.C. on the manner in which America's electronic media cover stories on drugs. The study revealed that between September 1989 and June 1990, 1,336 camera shots were taken for drug stories. Although African Americans comprised approximately 12 to 15 percent of the nation's population, they appeared in nearly 50 percent of camera shots. However, Whites, who according to the National Institute on Drug Abuse comprise the majority of America's drug users, were seen in only 32 percent of camera shots. A mixture of races were shown in 17 percent of the camera shots.

Reliable studies have been conducted on the types of stories print and electronic media cover about the African American community. These studies have revealed that a disturbingly high percentage of media coverage in the African American community is about crime and violence. The so-called liberal media establishment will quickly deny that they conspire to criminalize the image of Black people. But even if there is not an organized media conspiracy to criminalize the Black image, media practices have that effect.

The results of a USA Today/CNN Gallup poll contained in the October 28, 1993 issue of *USA Today* give a firm indication of the degree to which television news influences American perceptions of crime in America. It reported that 70 percent of Whites and 58 percent of Blacks surveyed feel their local television news accurately reflects the amount of crime in their area.

What this survey suggests is that the majority of Whites, and more than half of Blacks, accept the misinformation and false imagery television news promotes and projects about Black crime.

A more accurate instrument of crime measurement in the United States is the National Crime Survey (NCS). In its 1987 survey, the NCS reported that 66 percent of violent crime victims said their assailant was White; only 26.3 percent identified their assailant as Black, and 7.7 percent reported other or unknown. Jackie Mason was thoroughly misinformed when he commented: "By far the majority of any kind of violence that's taking place in this country, happens to be coming from the black community."

Moreover, the most heinous crimes in America have been committed by Whites. Even excluding the crimes of human enslavement, territorial robbery and the murder of millions of Native American and Africans, Whites are trend setters in crime. Consider America's serial killers—Ted Bundy, Charles Manson, Henry Lee Lucas, Ottis Toole, John Wayne Gacy, Jr., David Berkowitz, Jeffrey Dahmer and Wayne Williams; only Williams is African American. In *Hunting Humans* Michael Newton estimates that Whites comprise 85 percent of serial murderers in America.

In a January 1992 *USA Today* magazine article entitled *The Myth of Black Violence*, Dr. Evan Stark wrote:

> Self-report studies of youth give a completely different picture than figures on arrest or incarceration. The National Youth Survey of 1,725 youths 11-17 years of age whose self-reported, law-violating behavior was determined by confidential interviews found that "no significant race differences were found in any of the violent or serious offense scales.

The notions and images of African Americans as the most destructive and violent people in the United States are not consistent with what is really happening throughout this nation in terms of crime and violence.

MYTH #2
THE DRUG PROBLEM IS FAR MORE
PERVASIVE IN THE BLACK COMMUNITY

The African American community is plagued by adversities stemming from a significant number of its members abusing legal and illegal drugs. This essay is not an attempt to minimize the seriousness of drug abuse in the African American community. It merely aims to paint an accurate picture of drug abuse in America. The portrait of drug abuse in America is painted with long and broad "Black strokes." African Americans must not allow the existence of drug abuse in their community to be singled out and used for purposes that favor political elitists and others in the White supremacy structure.

Ironically William Bennett, former drug czar under the conservative Bush administration, helps dispel the myth of Black drug abuse in America. He described the typical cocaine user in America as a White male with a high school diploma who works full-time and lives in the suburbs[3]. This is a strikingly different description of the typical cocaine user than most Americans probably envision.

A University of Michigan study released in 1994 called *Monitoring the Future* revealed that drug use among eighth to twelfth graders is lowest among African Americans. The National Household Survey on Drug Abuse Report for 1992 revealed that 8.7 million Whites used drugs in one month versus 1.6 million Blacks.

The National Institute on Drug Abuse revealed that approximately 75 million Americans have used illegal drugs before—only 9 million, or 12 percent, were Black. More than 70 percent of drug users in America are White. While it is true that the problem of drug abuse in the African American community is serious, the perception that it is the American cesspool of drug abuse is false.

MYTH # 3
BLACK-ON-BLACK VIOLENCE IS THE SINGLE GREATEST THREAT TO THE SURVIVABILITY OF THE BLACK COMMUNITY

One of the fundamental philosophies of *The Seduction of Black Criminality* is that "Black-on-Black" violence is a form of Black self-degradation generated by centuries of psychological, cultural and physical degradation. (This issue is dealt with in the essay entitled *Oppressive Strategies that Seduce Blacks into Crime.)* However, I fully understand why many African Americans feel "Black-on-Black" violence is the greatest threat to Black survivability. The visual impact of Black bodies lying in the street dead from bullets fired by another Black person can have a bitter impact on the mind and emotions. However, perception is not always reality.

The notion that history will record that Blacks in America were destroyed through intra-racial violence discounts the destructive effects of the Maafa. The term Maafa refers to the great disaster of the African people, i.e., the Middle Passage—the torturous voyage from Africa to the West Indies—and the more than 240 years of chattel slavery. Much of the crime and violence seen in the African American community are consequences of the Maafa. Therefore, its unresolved legacy must be considered an equal factor—if not the greatest—in terms of threats to Black American survivability.

The combination of contemporary social and economic factors, and the political swing to the radical right, pose a greater threat to Black survivability than "Black-on-Black" violence. Consider the factor of Black victimization by police. In a study guide released by the United States Department of

14

Justice, National Institute of Justice entitled *Deadly Force* reports that:

> In Chicago, 70 percent of the civilians struck by police bullets were black, 20 percent were white, and 10 percent were hispanic. Data for Philadelphia, New York City, and Los Angeles reveal similar distributions.

Many officers are justified in resorting to shooting Black suspects. However, many African American communities can recall a number of tragic situations where Blacks were killed because police used force that was not necessary. In my native city, Milwaukee, Wisconsin, we remember the Ernest Lacy tragedy; Miami, Florida remembers the Arthur McDuffie tragedy; Jackson, Mississippi remembers the Dorothy Brown tragedy; New York City remembers the Eleanor Bumpurs tragedy, and many more can be cited.

Economic conditions in the African American community also pose a serious threat to Black survivability. The National Urban League's State of Black America 1989 report helps us understand. Information contained in an article entitled *The Economic Status of Black America* revealed that the median family income for Blacks in 1970 was $18,378—but the median family income for Whites was $29,960. In 1978, the median family income for Blacks rose slightly to $18,952—but Whites saw a greater rise to $31,998. In 1987, the median family income for Blacks dropped below the 1970 median to $18,098—but for Whites it had risen to $32,274.

If this trend continues, African Americans will never obtain economic parity with Whites, and it will become increasingly difficult for them to provide for themselves, especially in this cold political climate.

Myths about Black criminality and crime in the Black community have had profound psychological, political and economic effects on the African American community. Listed are 12 ways the African American community has been adversely affected by myths of Black criminality:

- Myths generate false perceptions of Black offenders and Blacks in general; this contributes to the negative perception the world has of Blacks in America, and more importantly, the negative perception many Blacks have of themselves.

- People consider Black crime to be more threatening than it actually is; this overshadows the claims raised by Blacks of unequal justice, economic deprivation, an inadequate education system, etc.

- Myths justify discourse to relax certain Constitutional rights in urban communities. Even African Americans become more willing to see certain guaranteed Constitutional rights relaxed so that police may have greater freedom to detain and search. In essence, people see violating the Constitutional rights of inner-city dwellers a necessity in order to handle what they perceive as rampant menacing crime and violence.

- Civil rights issues pertaining to Blacks receive less support from the mainstream political institution; and the larger society view civil rights issues that pertain to Blacks as low- or no-priority issues.

- Myths justify cuts and rollbacks of programs designed to provide Blacks with resources and avenues by which they can achieve and maintain social parity.

- Myths help create two brands of justice in America—one for Whites, another for Blacks. The law is enforced more aggressively in the African American community than in the White community. And the court system reacts more harshly to African Americans than Whites.

- Myths help create the notion that violence is a natural part of Black culture. This opinion affects how African American parents rear their children, particularly boys, how police respond to violent Black criminals, and how prisons treat Black inmates.

- Myths push major corporations out of "crime infested inner-cities" to seek peace in the suburbs, and discourage large corporate and small business development in inner cities, which prevents inner-city economic growth.

- Myths are used to legitimize White domination. White liberals, in the name of humanitarianism, control certain aspects of the African American social system, i.e., social service. This is because myths generate the attitude that African Americans are incapable of resolving their problems.

- Myths are one ingredient of a recipe for distrust and animosity in the African American community; they create class and ideological divisions within African American communities. This is in part due to the "we are our worst enemy" complex many Blacks suffer.

- Myths cause some non-Blacks to peg Blacks as criminal, or criminals that have not been caught. This produces widespread public suspicions of Blacks which manifests through merchants trailing Blacks around businesses; store security keeping closer surveillance on Blacks; White women clutching their purses and locking their car doors at the sight of a Black male; police being more likely to arrest Blacks than Whites who have committed the same crime.

This list underscores that myths should not be viewed as mere pieces of inconsequential false information. It also sheds light on how racial myths aimed at Blacks are used to keep them under control.

CRIME HANDS BLACK AMERICA A HIGH TAB

There is another matter that begs our attention. This matter develops out of the promotion of lies and half truths about Black crime and the projection of criminalized Black images. African Americans can anticipate suffering harsh repercussions of White misperception. Many Whites incorrectly think Black crime is the most serious threat to their safety, and that it is the most expensive item on the "tab" crime hands America.

The cost of crime in America is far greater than most people realize. The December 13, 1993 issue of *Business Week* magazine contains an article entitled "The Cost of Crime in America." This article focuses on the amount of money spent and lost as a result of medical care, property loss, urban decay, private protection, the criminal justice system, and lives shattered by crime. The one great flaw of this article is that the massive cost of white-collar crime is not factored into the equation. Observe the estimated cost of these six items listed and their astronomical total cost:

Medical Care	$5 Billion
Property Loss	$45 Billion
Urban Decay	$50 Billion
Private Protection	$65 Billion
Criminal Justice	$90 Billion
Shattered Lives	$170 Billion
TOTAL COST	**$425 Billion**

Are African Americans affected by a $425 billion tab for crime in America? Yes! Consider the superficial circumstances. African Americans comprise approximately 12 to 15 percent of the American population while being represented in greater percentages in the criminal justice institution. According to the study guides entitled *Jail Inmates, and Prisoners*, released by the Bureau of Justice Statistics, Blacks represent 47 percent of inmates in jail awaiting or serving sentences, and more than 45 percent of state and federal inmates. All together there are more than 1,000,000 Blacks imprisoned and on probation and parole[4].

The actual seriousness of crime in the African American community and related myths, coupled with the astronomical cost of crime in America, are causing White animosity and intolerance toward African Americans to mount. Whites are becoming less interested in the needs and concerns of African Americans. They are weary of watching billions of their tax dollars go down the "criminal justice drain" to arrest, jail, prosecute, imprison and supervise Blacks. The fact that the disproportionate number of Black arrests, prosecutions, jail and prison inmates are the result of discrimination and racism is immaterial. Blacks must pay. And Blacks are paying this tab. The criminal justice system has shifted into overdrive with regard to crime in the African American community. It is worth noting that this shift occurred while the national political leadership was overwhelmingly liberal. It goes without saying that the "Gingrification" of national politics will lead to even harsher responses from the justice system.

The justice system's shift into "overdrive justice" can be seen in juvenile justice. Juveniles who are convicted of committing serious crimes are being certified as adults in alarming numbers. There is discussion in some states about lowering the age for adult certification. The trend of adult certification is moving in a frightening direction with regard to Blacks. Former Tarrant County Assistant District Attorney Renee Harris observed over her nearly eight-year tenure with the District Attorney's office that there was a "marked increase of juveniles being certified as adults, the majority of which were Black."

Americans are becoming more comfortable with the idea of relaxing restrictions placed on police by the Constitution in certain "high crime areas"—a euphemistic term for urban Black communities. Numerous local, state and federally sponsored crime initiatives that have emerged over recent years with catchy names, but in many ways these programs are harmful to segments of the African American community.

The Federal Violence Initiative is a chilling example of what mainstream science has in store for those it considers to be genetically bent toward violence. The Federal Violence Initiative was a project presented to the National Mental Health Advisory Council in 1992 by Dr. Frederick Goodwin—the government's highest-ranking psychiatrist at that time. This project involved identifying 100,000 inner-city children whose "biochemical" and "genetic" defects will cause them to become violent later in life. The children were to be treated in special day camps, given counseling for behavior modification in the family, and psychoactive drugs. The efforts of the Congressional Black Caucus (CBC), led by Representative John Conyers, resulted in Goodwin's resignation. However, shortly after his resignation Goodwin was designated to head the National Institute of Mental Health.

The mass media's feeding frenzy over Black crime, the promotion of lies and half truths—myths—about crime in the Black community, and the astronomical cost of crime in America generate White hysteria. Moreover, they justify the abuse of Black people, and White control over America's social, political and economic systems.

Two

White Domination, Black Criminality

This problem of racism, which we see all around the world in such evil manifestations, is a problem right here in the United States of America that can destroy this country unless we all find a way as a nation to deal with it . . . If you look at the overall causes of violence and violent crimes, racism in our society is a huge continuing cause.

Vice President Al Gore
BET Lead Story Interview, February 1994

The ensemble of Black crime, myths of Black crime, mass media's criminalization of the Black image, and the promotion of lies and half truths about crime in the Black community serve a vital function in the American social system. They are the instruments used by the ruling elite to maintain control over the African American community and the American social system.

The Charles Stuart incident demonstrates one way in which this process can operate. On October 23, 1989, Charles Stuart reported to Boston police that a man shot him and his pregnant wife in a robbery, killing her. He told police that the perpetrator was a Black man. The results were horrendous. The news media reacted with their usual feeding frenzy, state politicians began ranting and raving about resurrecting the death penalty, and the police went into high gear in three of Boston's predominantly African American communities in search of the murderer. The hunt for the Stuart murderer culminated with the arrest of a Black man named William Bennett. The police talked as though they were certain Bennett was the murderer. However, Boston police received a call from Charles Stuart's brother, Matthew. Matthew told police that Charles Stuart committed the murder. Before Stuart could be arrested, he killed himself by jumping off a bridge. Matthew's story was not a lie[5].

21

Although the real murderer was discovered and Bennett was vindicated, numerous Black males in Boston had been criminalized and had their Constitutional rights violated by police. The discussion in the Massachusetts legislature about reinstating the death penalty, the ruthless policing of Black males, and the illegal arrest of William Bennett were legitimized by White hysteria over sensationalized violent Black crime, lies and half truths about crime in the Black community, and the potent "little white lie" Charles Stuart told.

This is not the first time a White offender has cried "Black!" to manipulate investigative attention. The annals of American history are littered with scores of similar tragedies. One of the most recent was the October, 1994 Susan Smith double murder case. Susan Smith was a White woman in Union, South Carolina, who strapped her two sons, Michael, 3, and Alex, 14 months, in the seat of her vehicle and rolled it into a lake, drowning them.

Smith crafted a wickedly cunning story that she was car-jacked by a Black man in his 20s. She said he drove her and her two sons about ten miles outside of town, ordered her out of the vehicle, then drove off with her two sons still inside. Frantic local townspeople, police, state troopers, helicopters and the FBI combed the entire county searching for the vehicle and the children. Shortly after going on television and making a tearful plea to the nonexistent Black car-jacker to return her boys unharmed, Smith admitted that she murdered her two sons[6]. Smith assumed that by blaming the "the national crook" she would strike a cord of fear in the heart of America and crush any suspicions that she murdered her sons. The scheme failed this time, but it has worked countless times before.

MEDIA AND THE HISTORICAL ROLE OF BLACK CRIME IN AMERICA

Black criminality's role in the American social system has not changed since 1619. History overflows with demonstrations that Black criminality has functioned to justify the abuse and exploitation of Blacks, and the maintenance of White control over the American social system.

Since the inception of the media establishment, one of its roles has been to arm the ruling elite with justification to oppress African Americans and control the social system without being ridiculed by the world. Its projections of false images and promotion of misinformation about Blacks serve as controlling devices.

The media project two dominant images of Blacks. When Blacks do not fit into one of these two categories, it is difficult for them to flag the media's attention. The first image is the sensual and exotic creature, such as the sexy entertainer or the spectacular athlete. The second is the angry and destructive beast, such as the violent criminal or the political militant.

The media sensationalize Black crime and habitually dwell on certain tragic incidents without end. In his book, *Unreliable Sources*, Lee Martin discusses the results of a study on media coverage conducted by Kirk Johnson in two of Boston's African American communities. Martin quotes Johnson as follows:

> Most of the stories about these neighborhoods dealt with crime or violent accidents and, all in all, 85 percent reinforced negative stereotypes of blacks. Blacks were persistently shown as drug pushers and users, as thieves, as troublemakers, and as victims or perpetrators of violence.

These kinds of media practices incite White hysteria over Black crime. They generate the idea that America's crime crisis exists primarily because Blacks exist. Moreover, they cause Black crime to become a magnet that draws national attention to serious crime issues in America. The media's intense coverage of former World Heavyweight Boxing Champion Mike Tyson brought the issue of date rape to the fore of national interest; its spotlight on pop star Michael Jackson drew national attention to child sexual abuse; its feeding frenzy over the Anita Hill/Clarence Thomas hearings elevated sexual harassment in the workplace to a level of interest it never had—even conservative Clarence Thomas referred to is treatment as a "high-tech lynching"—; and its insane coverage of football legend, actor, and sports commentator Orenthal James Simpson caused the nation to view domestic abuse as a more deplorable crime than it had prior to his becoming the suspect in the Nicole Simpson/Ronald Goldman murders.

What is interesting about these situations is that they involved Black men who were basically admired and "acceptable" to the larger society. Mike Tyson probably is the only exception. However, there is no doubt in my mind that between Jackson, Thomas and Simpson, "The Juice" was the most "acceptable." His crossover appeal coupled with his good ole American boy persona made Whites comfortable with Simpson. Add to that his athletic prowess, attractive build, gorgeous smile, and natural charisma and you have the ingredients of the "All-American guy." However, Simpson's All-American guy status and White American acceptability did not whiten his Black skin when he became suspected of having murdered two White people. The media rushed to hang O.J.'s dirty laundry on the "media clothes line" for the world to behold. Moreover, many television polls revealed that most Whites thought good ole O.J. was guilty. Had the murder victims been Black, media interest in this case would have been short-lived. Its response to the O.J. incident is another clear testament to a fact known to many African Americans. In America it does not matter how fast a Black person can run with a ball, how well they can sing and dance, how wealthy they are, nor how deeply they have assimilated into the larger culture—when they commit a crime, or are suspected of the same, the media draw little distinction between them and the Black thief in the ghetto.

The image of the angry and destructive Black beast, Black male especially, is part of the rational basis the dominant culture stands on to oppress Blacks. It also provides them with a justification to exclude the collective African American community from fully participating on every level of every major institution in America.

D.W. Griffith's 1915 Civil War epic, *The Birth of a Nation*, is a fitting cinematic example of Black aggression being exaggerated and used by Whites as a rationale to abuse Blacks and control the nation. In his book, *Blacks in American Film and Television*, Donald Bogle calls *The Birth of a Nation*: "A legendary classic, a racist masterpiece." In this production, all is calm and peaceful in Piedmont, South Carolina until the Civil War breaks out. Then a Negro uprising results in the demise of White rule in the South.

The South then becomes a place where "lawlessness runs riot." Negro slaves abandon the plantation fields to dance in the streets; they romp around the city rudely pushing and shoving Whites about. The Negros gain control of Congress through stuffing the ballots with extra votes. And during a Congressional session, they chomp on fried chicken, drink whiskey and place their foul-smelling feet on the desks.

White tolerance nearly snaps when a lust-filled Negro named Gus chases the daughter of the honorable Dr. Cameron to a cliff. The young woman loses her life when she leaps off the cliff into the "opal gates of death." But when a mulatto man named Silas Lynch attempts to force a White woman named Elsie Stoneman into marriage, the White South can tolerate no more. Griffith's solution to Black rule and brutality comes in the form of three letters—KKK. A group of White males adorned in white hoods and sheets attack and subdue the rapacious Negros and regain control of the South. This gives birth to the nation.

The Birth of a Nation caused the oppression of Black males to appear righteous and correct by portraying them as sex-crazed menaces to Southern society, and the murderous Ku Klux Klan gang as messiahs of the South. It is frightening that today Black males are being portrayed as menaces to society as they were in the era of *The Birth of a Nation*. Some fear that today the stage is being set for increased Black oppression.

BLACK DYSFUNCTIONALITY: A REQUISITE FOR WHITE DOMINATION

A simple but illuminating lesson about White domination in America and the world can be learned through American slavery. The main motivation for the enslavement of Africans by Whites was the false religious ideology that emerged out of the Catholic Church, which considered Africans "infidels." In the fifteenth century, the Pope authorized Spain and Portugal to capture and enslave Africans on the grounds that they were infidels and therefore needed to be Christianized. Two centuries later, the European slave system was introduced into the "New World."

American slavery did not start off as the inhumane and brutal system that we know it was. The mid-1660s marked the moment in American history when chattel slavery became inhumane and brutal. Is there an explanation for this transformation? Yes. Slavery had become a major source of income in America since its legalization, particularly in the South. By the late 1600s, Whites had a vested financial interest in this institution. This interest was threatened by the tenacious spirit of the enslaved African.

In order to maintain this institution and keep profits high, the African spirit had to be crushed. The enslaved had to be made dependent on the plantation owner and accepting of the exploitative system of American slavery. This was not an easy task. Plantation owners were met with firm resistance by many enslaved Africans. The plantation owners saw in the breakdown of the African personality the means by which they could cultivate African acceptance of dehumanizing enslavement. Plantation owners facilitated this breakdown by viciously attacking African bodies, character and culture[7]. Whites would not have been able to control Africans for 246 years had the African personality not been fractured through the most cruel attacks on the bodies, culture and character of Africans.

The romanticized songs of Southern slavery, and the pictures of glowing slaves skinnin' and grinnin' in the wind-blown cotton fields are so far from the truth that they are almost abominable. Many Africans vigorously fought and resisted slavery to the point of death. In *American Negro Slave Revolts*, Herbert Aptheker records 250 revolts and conspiracies initiated by enslaved Africans in the eighteenth century alone. African resistance of oppression was so intense in that century that it was called "the century of resistance."

To ensure the maintenance of African enslavement, Whites designed strategies and utilized tactics that cultivated confusion, relational disorder and dysfunctionalities in the African slave culture and personality. The illuminating lesson to be learned from American slavery is that in order to successfully oppress a people, they must become dysfunctional.

A PRESCRIPTION FOR OPPRESSION

It is not immoral for a particular racial or ethnic group to control their economic and political system. This type of control is a noble social concept known as nationalism. However, when a particular racial or ethnic group within a nation endeavors to control the social, political and economic systems of other groups within that nation, or the world, it is immoral. The global White elite have been plotting to control the social, political and economic systems of other groups in the world for more than 500 years. They have incited social disorder in many non-White territories throughout the world to attain control.

Ironically, it was the highest-ranking member of the Catholic Church who sanctioned the European movement to bring Africans into servitude. In the 1400s, the Pope authorized warring Spain and Portugal to capture Africans and reduce them to servants. Two centuries later, Europeans began importing Africans into the "New World" from the West Coast of Africa.

White American capitalists then exploited African labor for more than 240 years. When slavery was abolished, White capitalists further exploited African labor through two massive revenue-generating systems called peonage and workgangs. This was followed by another system of Black social control called Jim Crow.

Africans in America suffered severely inhumane types of treatment in a society that touted itself as the leader of democracy, the land of liberty and justice for all. African American oppression occurred because the ideologies of White nationalism and White supremacy were intermingled. (It is quite a thought that African Americans have only been a free people— that is without any legally enforceable social restraints—a little more than 25 years.)

Whites employed the most heinous strategies to maintain control over Africans in America. They included brainwashing, creating classism, family separation, inferiorization, mental and emotional terrorization, incredible physical brutality and murder. They were not concerned with Black pain and agony. The physical and psychological pain and cultural damage caused by harsh oppression was a necessity in order that White social, political and economic dominance could be maintained in America.

DENIAL AND THE POLITICS OF STATUS QUO

The debate continues to wage over whether one generation of "freedom" and "equal opportunity" is sufficient time for African Americans to recover from 350 years of oppression. Many Whites become agitated when their parents' violent and inhumane treatment of Blacks is presented as a factor contributing to the problems of Blacks today. Their general attitude is: "Don't blame me for your problems . . . I didn't have anything to with what my grandparents did."

Whites are quick to remind Blacks that slavery was abolished "a long time ago" and they are not slaves today. However, their historical amnesia prevents them from remembering that Jim Crow/legal segregation was alive 30 years ago. Blacks were brutally beaten, lynched and murdered with impunity during this era. Certain nefarious law enforcement programs that brought the destruction of Black political organizations and facilitated the murder of Black leaders have not been terminated more than a generation. Institutional racism has many Blacks marginalized, and the psychic pain of racism is yet felt by Blacks today. Nonetheless, Whites tend to discount the negative impact of these harsh experiences.

26

Total recovery from past oppression would still have been unattainable even if African Americans had received genuine equality, opportunity and justice over the last 25 years. But African Americans continue to struggle against inequality, lack of opportunity and injustice. This struggle persists because White racism was not eradicated when African Americans were supposedly mainstreamed into society. To solely blame African Americans for their numerous problems, without factoring in their oppressive treatment, both past and present, is the epitome of blaming the victim.

It is necessary for Whites to deny that African American oppression factors into current African American problems. Conceding to this point would be an indirect admission that Whites contribute to the problems of African American people. It would also be difficult to dismantle programs designed to repair the damage caused by past oppression and create avenues by which African Americans can attain parity with the larger society. The existence of meaningful measures to aid the collective African American community in their recovery from the devastations of White racism works against the supreme goal of the White ruling elite, which is the maintenance of their social control.

The ruling elite has failed to demonstrate to African Americans in a convincing way that it wants to open doors of political and economic opportunity to Blacks, not just some Blacks, so that they can build power. However, it has demonstrated that it will employ the most immoral measures to maintain its dominance. It will order the placement of "legal traps" in African American communities that capture the guilty and innocent. It increases in power through significant numbers of African Americans being stamped with the label criminal. Social environments are engineered, information is promoted, and images are projected that degrade African Americans and cultivate Black self-hatred, which manifests itself in the form of "Black-on-Black" violence. Prison systems are constructed that discourage genuine rehabilitation and encourage Black criminalization for the purpose of exploiting labor.

Many Whites think [White] racism was virtually eradicated during the late '60s and early '70s. People who believe this generally assume that if White racism is present in America, it is mainly seen in rural areas where "radical" racist organizations are headquartered. However, this is not consistent with what Blacks are experiencing in America. Nor is it consistent with what some experts are saying. In *Hate Crimes*, sociologist Jack Levin, and Jack McDevitt a leading academic expert on hate crimes in America, state:

Most hate crimes do not involve organized hate groups, whose members are dedicated to the goal of achieving racial purity. Perpetrators usually are not card-carrying members of any racist organizations; they do not wear uniforms, armbands, or sheets . . .

27

Hate crimes are more often committed under ordinary circumstances by otherwise unremarkable types—neighbors, a co-worker at the next desk, or groups of youngsters looking for a thrill.

Many individuals who subscribe to the thought that White racism is virtually non-existent in the United States base their belief on the fact that the state sponsored institution of Jim Crow segregation was dismantled. They suggest that its dismantling swung open the doors of mainstream American society, offering African Americans a world of opportunity.

The logic therefore is that since the signs that blatantly barred Blacks from certain segments of society are no longer posted, and because Whites generally refrain from calling African Americans nigger to their faces, and police brutality is not as bad as it used to be, African Americans should be shouting glory in the streets. Derrick Bell speaks to this matter in his book *Faces At The Bottom Of The Well*, Bell writes:

Contemporary color barriers are certainly less visible as a result of our successful effort to strip the law's endorsement from the hated Jim Crow signs. Today one can travel for thousands of miles across the country and never see a public facility designated as "Colored" or "White." Indeed, the very absence of visible signs of discrimination creates an atmosphere of racial neutrality and encourages Whites to believe that racism is a thing of the past.

The collapse of legally enforced Jim Crow segregation had no effect on White attitudes toward Blacks. American culture remained passionately anti-Black. America had become so naturally racist—oriented to keep Whites in a superior social position—it did not need a structure for racism to operate on. The collapse of Jim Crow did not tame the media beast that craves sensational Black crime, nor did it stop the flow of pseudo-science that demeaned Black character.

Doors into mainstream society were open to African Americans, however; White gatekeepers maintained limits on the number of African Americans that came through them. An ABC *Primetime Live* show that aired on November 26, 1992 showed the White gatekeepers at work. It was called *True Colors*. This show focused on an experiment conducted in St. Louis, Missouri that utilized two testers, one Black, one White, with identical credentials and backgrounds. They were placed in a number of different settings to determine how close America was to being a race-neutral, color-blind society. The results of this 2.5 week experiment permit us to see racism in action.

John, the White tester, inquired about an apartment rental in a predominantly White neighborhood. He was provided a key by the White landlord and permitted to observe the apartment unaccompanied. Minutes after John left, Glen, the Black tester, arrived and inquired about the same apartment. The same landlord told him the apartment was not available. The testers were sent to a car dealership. The salesman quoted Glen a price of $9,500 with a 20 to 25 percent down-payment required. Shortly afterwards, John was sent in and the same salesman quoted him a price of $9,000 with a 10 to 20 percent down-payment required for the same vehicle.

Research groups have conducted a number of studies on racism. They reveal that race-based bias and discrimination does exist in every segment of American society. Nonetheless, United States Representative Newt Gingrich and the GOP insist on rolling back affirmative action, asserting that it discriminates against Whites, particularly White males. Rush Limbaugh suggests affirmative action says to Blacks: "You can't do it without some help." Doing it is not the problem Mr. Limbaugh, having the opportunity to do it is.

There are two fundamental reasons that Whites deny or avoid the reality of racism/White supremacy in America. First, they want to be able to say that African Americans are solely responsible for their problems. Second, they remain guilt-free with the thought of an America free of White racism. Many Whites would simply be emotionally shattered if they fully realized that America is not one nation under God with "liberty and justice for all."

The question we must ask ourselves is: What is racism? Psychiatrist Dr. Frances Cress Welsing offers her definition of racism. In her book entitled *The Isis Papers*, Welsing states:

> The Color-Confrontation theory states that the white or color-deficient Europeans responded psychologically, with a profound sense of numerical inadequacy and color inferiority, in their confrontations with the majority of the world's people — all of whom possessed varying degrees of color-producing capacity. This psychological response, whether conscious or unconscious, revealed an inadequacy based on the most obvious and fundamental part of their being, their external appearance. As might be anticipated in terms of modern psychological theories, whites defensively developed an uncontrollable sense of hostility and aggression. This attitude has continued to manifest itself throughout the history of mass confrontations between whites and people of color.

Dr. Welsing's *Theory of Color-Confrontation and Racism* describes the evolution of racism and what the fully developed animal is. The *Cress Theory of Color-Confrontation and Racism* explains that the European response to their fear of genetic annihilation, minority status in the world, and lack of skin color (melanin) was the creation of the devilish philosophy that non-Whites were inferior to them. This philosophy was a driving force behind the European quest to control the world's non-White population.

Racism essentially is the practice of White control over non-Whites, which is motivated by the erroneous belief that non-Whites are inferior to them. It is incorrect to assume that racism is simply one race mistreating another. The central component of racism is the ability to control another race. Therefore, since African Americans do not possess the power to control other races, they cannot be racist. Hate does come in many colors. However, what many people consider Black racism is actually Black reactions to White racism.

WHITE RACISM BREEDS BLACK CRIME

The *Cress Theory of Color-Confrontation and Racism* explains that the fear of genetic annihilation is a key ingredient of White racism. The group that possesses the greatest potential to genetically eliminate Whites are Blacks, particularly Black males. The fear of genetic elimination creates White animosity toward Black males. This emotion factored into the savage murder of a 14-year-old Black boy in Mississippi named Emmett Till. Till allegedly committed an act Whites made criminal for Black males to do— whistle at a White woman. White men simply were consumed with fear that Black men were going to color them out of the picture. Because Black men possess the greatest potential to eliminate Whites, they wear the title "public enemy number one."

The castration of Black male genitalia, an act which occurred regularly during chattel slavery and frequently during the first three decades of the 1900s, was a direct attack on the "weapon" of White elimination. Blacks have historically suffered the most malevolent attacks by the White supremacy system. The attacks have been ruthless and thorough encompassing the mind, body, spirit and culture of Black people. Racism causes Whites to discount Black pain. It should not be surprising that Whites today depreciate the effects of centuries of heinous Black oppression.

The human personality is durable, the African personality in particular. However, its durability does not mean that it will not be adversely affected by tremendous hardship. When humans are subjected to unhealthy conditions, particularly long-term, they will demonstrate unhealthy behaviors. Black crime and violence are unhealthy effects of long-term subjection to unhealthy conditions.

Mainstream criminology cites a laundry list of causes of Black crime and violence. Some include poverty, joblessness, community breakdown, family breakdown, drugs, poor education, and outlandish causes such as biology, genetics, a criminal personality, brain composition, etc. These variables do contribute to Black crime and violence. But they are likewise effects of long-term Black oppression.

Black authors, lecturers, radio and television hosts and publishers of news are saturating the Black community with a wealth of liberating information. At the same time philosophers, media personalities, psychologists and psychiatrists are peddling lies and half truths about Blacks and Black sociology to shatter any notions that Black crime is linked to White racism. They aim to convince the American people, Whites in particular, that Black people's grievances about America are ill-founded because their problem is themselves.

WHITE RACISM: A ROOT CAUSE, NOT A WEAK EXCUSE

The idea that Black crime is linked to White racism should not be interpreted to mean that racism is the only reason Blacks engage in crime. However, it is a root cause. The degrading acts of violence seen in African American communities are the product of centuries of Black victimization through degrading White violence. It is common for victims to exhibit the behavior of their victimizer. Two-thirds of all violent offenders in prison were physically assaulted as children. The notion that the effects of 350 years of Black victimization can be filtered out in 25 years is asinine.

Crime and violence in the Black community are "fruits of oppression." Apple trees bear apples; likewise, oppression bears oppressive fruit. This concept is underscored in history. Dr. Earl Hutchinson offers us historical evidence affirming that there is a connection between White racism and Black criminality. In *The Mugging of Black America*, Hutchinson writes:

> Researchers compared homicide rates among ethnic groups in West and East Africa to Philadelphia blacks. The American black murder rate was 600 times greater than the African.

Dr. Hutchinson offers more historical evidence to support the position that Black criminal and violent behaviors are fruits of oppression. He later wrote:

> All black towns in the South where white control was at a minimum had the lowest crime rates. Mound Bayou, Mississippi did not record a single murder during the 1920s. Boley, Oklahoma had the lowest crime rate in the state during the 1940s. The picture drastically changed when white administration and law took over.

A self-destructive Black community serves White supremacy in America. One in three African American males in their 20s being supervised by the criminal justice system strengthens the White supremacy structure. African American males do not commit most of the crime in America, but they occupy a large share of America's prison beds. If others are committing more crime than they, why are there more African American males in prison? This maintains White domination. Black males pose a serious threat to

31

White domination. They are therefore targeted by society and the criminal justice system. Criminalization is a potent weapon to socially castrate Black men. White domination and Black criminality relate in two ways: White domination generates Black crime, and Black crime maintains White domination.

THREE

OPPRESSIVE STRATEGIES THAT SEDUCE BLACKS INTO CRIME

The first operation of the seduction machination entails the criminalization of Blacks in America through seducing them into crime through abuse. Many Whites consider Black oppression an excuse Blacks use to be lazy and commit crime instead of work. They say this without even possessing a basic knowledge of Black oppression. In fact, they do not want to know about it. Many Whites are not aware of the heinous psychomanipulative strategies that were employed to control Africans in America. The violence being exhibited in the African American community is the legacy of these heinous strategies. Many Whites are blinded by denial and avoidance. Denial and avoidance render the Maafa inconsequential with regard to contemporary Black behavior and social circumstances. Whites who are in denial and avoidance assert that if adverse carryovers do exist, they are minimal at best.

The degrading attack on Black personality has urged Blacks into a vicious cycle of self-degradation. This attack extends from the European invasion of Africa through the era of institutional racism that began in the late '60s. Blacks were socialized into self-degradation through long-term victimization by a variety of abusive tactics. These tactics were utilized by Whites for three main purposes. First, to break down the African personality, making them dependent on Whites. Second, to make Africans controllable, thus ensuring White American economic and political control. Third, so Whites could attain tremendous wealth through the exploitation of nonresistant African labor.

Discussion and study are in progress to determine if Black crime is the product of Black people possessing a "criminal personality." Black crime definitely is not the product of "criminal personalities." It is the product of personalities damaged and corrupted by the activities of politically and economically "criminal societies."

Many Whites disregard or greatly discount society's role in the production of Black crime. There are likewise a number of African Americans who choose to disregard or discount its role. Some of these people will not implicate society because they have adopted racist opinions. Others are fearful that they would be giving Blacks a "license to kill." They fail to understand that it is possible to discuss the role of society in the creation of Black crime without suggesting that Black oppression justifies Black criminality.

THE MANIPULATION OF THE WILL

Many Blacks say: "White people can't make Black folk do anything they do not want to do . . . whatever a Black person does they do it because they want to!" This moralistic remark sounds logical, but it is untrue. In *Black-on-Black Violence*, Dr. Amos Wilson writes:

> Criminal personalities, like all personalities, are to a significant degree socially created and defined. Their behavioral characters can only be manifested within a social context. They therefore cannot stand outside social time, place, and circumstances. When a society looks into the face of its criminals it looks in a mirror and sees a reflection of its own likeness.

Dr. Wilson helps us understand that society is a co-creator of personalities and behaviors. It is therefore impossible to engage in meaningful conversations or studies of crime and violence outside of a sociological context. Eurocentric criminology tends to avoid bringing past or present sociological conditions into its focus of Black criminological study. Its focus tends to center on Black society and the individual Black criminal. Eurocentric criminologists attempt to sever society's relationship to Black crime and violence. Crime and society cannot be divorced. When studies aimed at determining the causes of crime and violence are conducted outside a sociological context, the results almost invariably point to the criminal, or to the group the criminal comes from. This explains why Eurocentric criminology generally finds causes for Black crime and violence that point almost exclusively to the failures of Black social institutions, or flaws within the Black criminal's personality. Some of these commonly cited causes include:

- family breakdown
- community breakdown
- unemployment
- poverty
- drugs
- lack of education
- male irresponsibility
- brain composition
- biochemistry
- genetic defects

It is curious that some Eurocentric criminologists cite "biochemical" and "genetic" defects as causes of Black crime. When Black crime and White crime are placed side by side, White crime has a far more reprehensible record than Black crime. However, Eurocentric criminologists generally do not consider biochemistry or genetics as causes of White crime.

The opinion that: "White people can't make Black folk do anything they do not want to do . . . whatever a Black person does they do it because they want to" affirms the Eurocentric theory of Black crime. This remark essentially says that every activity a human being engages in is driven completely by free will. This is not fully accurate. The human will is a major factor that drives human behavior. However, two facts must be considered. First, the human will is not inviolable. It can be broken and corrupted. Second, the human will is not the only factor driving human behavior. Basic human behavior teaches that the way to control a man's actions is to control his thoughts. The idea that our actions are driven solely by our will goes against the basic teachings of human behavior.

We must understand the process of "desire creation." Desire creation is the process where certain desires are produced within an individual as a result of their being mentally manipulated into perceiving something as absolutely necessary. Americans dump billions of dollars into the American marketplace as a result of desire creation. The marketplace employs an assortment of marketing and advertising tactics aimed at generating desire within consumers. Competitors actually engage in the "war of desire creation." The competitor who produces greater amounts of desire takes the spoils of high economic profits.

Businesses apply an effective principle to the production of commercials. It is called the principle of identification. Businesses pay athletes and entertainers millions of dollars to endorse their product because identifying their product with them almost invariably guarantees large profits. Commercials are produced that utilize physically attractive men and women, catchy phrases and positive slogans to reel consumers in by appealing to their egos and fantasies. Commercials sell sex appeal, vivaciousness, attractiveness, happiness, power and success, and people buy their product in hopes of attaining them.

Clearly the thought that every behavior that people engage in is determined wholly of their free will is a falsehood. The abhorrent violence seen in some African American communities is not the action of a people acting *wholly* on free will. To a large extent they are satisfying socially created self-destructive desires. These desires were created over centuries of oppression. Oppression causes Blacks to identify with their oppressor as a way of escaping the pain that comes with being in the oppressed group. However, an individual who identifies with the oppressor takes on the attitudes and values of the oppressor and models them. When the oppressed model the oppressor, they engage in self-abuse, i.e., "Black-on-Black" violence.

VIOLENCE BEGETS VIOLENCE

Whites have utilized an assortment of tactics to regulate Black behavior and maintain control of the American social system. African Americans have been subjected to degrading violence for more than 350 years, and this violence has placed them on the pathway of self-abuse.

The term "pathway of self-abuse" describes movement and progress. This is an accurate description, because Black violence waxed more egregious as time progressed. There are at least four explanations for this. First, violence in America waxed more egregious; therefore so has Black violence, since Black violence is connected to the whole culture of violence in America. Second, the collective African American community has never received post-trauma counseling to recover from oppression; the result— pockets of ever-worsening problems. Third, social variables are at work today that were nonexistent a century ago, i.e., the modern media. These variables produce a more intense drawing affect into violence. Fourth, African Americans are victims of a more intense onslaught of psychic violence. African Americans in the early 1900s experienced physical lynching, while African Americans in the late 1900s are experiencing a "lynching of the mind."

The types of violence committed against Blacks can be placed in three categories: 1) psychic, 2) physical and 3) cultural. These categories will be divided and explored in four separate phases. They are: 1) Trans-Atlantic slave trade, 2) slavery, 3) post-slavery and 4) post-segregation.

TRANS-ATLANTIC SLAVE TRADE PHASE
PSYCHIC, PHYSICAL AND CULTURAL VIOLENCE

The depth and intensity of emotional and psychological trauma Africans suffered as a result of the Trans-Atlantic slave trade can never be fully appreciated. Merely reflecting upon and exploring the details of this bitter experience is emotionally painful and mentally anguishing. However, the pain felt in studying this experience cannot be compared to the pain of its actual experience.

The journey to the West Indies was called the Middle Passage. It was precipitated by the abrupt invasion of African communities by gangs of armed marauders and brutal physical confrontations that brought death to scores of Africans of every age. The infrastructure of African communities was ravaged. Other Africans befriended visiting Europeans only to be betrayed and forced into captivity. The captives were shackled about their necks, hands and feet, and marched many miles in blistering heat to the Atlantic to be forced into the bowels of ships.

The Africans were packaged inside the smelly bowels of these ships in sardine-like conditions where they remained throughout the journey, which could last as long as two months. Death was a way of life in the Middle Passage conduit. Millions of Africans were murdered by bullet, knife, being tossed into the ocean to drown or to be mutilated by sharks. They slept and ate lying in their own urine and feces. In essence these ships were floating torture chambers. And these experiences were only the beginning of the African captive's pains and sorrows.

Upon arrival in the West Indies, the African captives were forced to endure a dehumanizing breaking process that involved the exercise of inhumane forms of physical, psychological and cultural violence. Africans were robbed of their names and forbidden to speak their native tongues. They were dehumanized by being told they evolved from beasts such as apes and gorillas. Africans who were considered "unbreakable" were often tortured and murdered in front of others to compel them into obedience. After being brutally beaten, tortured and starved into docility, the Africans were ready for auction.

Slave auctions humiliated and degraded Africans. They stood naked on platforms to be physically inspected from head to toe by prospective buyers. The pains of the Middle Passage, the breaking process, and the humiliation of auction would often be compounded with the abrupt separation of African families and friends. This left them with no familial or fraternal support systems. They felt the full brunt of emotional pain and suffering caused by oppression. The enslaved Africans were then transported from the West Indies to America and placed in the concentration camp of plantation slavery. They were "beastified" through animalistic treatment and responsibility.

SLAVERY PHASE
PSYCHIC, PHYSICAL AND CULTURAL VIOLENCE

Europeans were not the pioneers of human enslavement. In fact, slavery was introduced into the world centuries before Europe existed. Africans were familiar with slavery prior to the American slave system having practiced it in Africa. However, Africans were not familiar with the kind of slavery Europeans practiced in the "New World." In *Lessons From History*, Dr. Jawanza Kunjufu writes:

> Slavery has existed all over the world, and Africa is no exception. There were African slaves who helped build the pyramids. When the invaders arrived, they observed slavery. Slavery also existed in Asia and Europe. The African value system had a different meaning for slavery and war. Often African communities would engage in war, but the outcome was surrender, not death for the defeated group. For example, the Masai would surround the Gikuyu, establishing victory and then they would let the Gikuyu escape
>
> This same value system applied to slavery. A person could be a slave, but not suffer the extremes of psychological and physical brutality that were the norm in American slavery. African slavery did not include lynching, selling family members to different locations; nor was it a permanent existence for its slaves.

American slavery was a brutal, inhumane institution void of value and respect for the enslaved. The dehumanizing nature of American slavery incited a high level of resistance within the enslaved African community. It became necessary for plantation owners to utilize gross psychological and behavior-modifying tactics to generate an acceptance of this demoralizing kind of slavery within Africans.

Plantation owners "inferiorized" them through creating a slave culture that was thoroughly inferior to White culture. They were tagged with inferior labels such as nigger, housed in inferior structures, and forced to treat Whites as though they were superior. Every aspect of their lives screamed of their inferiority.

The plantation owners "de-Africanized" American-born enslaved Africans by degrading all things related to Africa and its culture. Hence, enslaved Africans began rejecting their homeland and the rich culture they once cherished.

Africans were not considered fully human. This legitimized their being starved, raped, hunted, tortured and murdered. The males were forced to engage in brutal fights with one another as entertainment for local plantation owners and their families. The females were reduced to instruments of sexual titillation and experimentation for the plantation owner and other White males. Although they had no control over the behavior of the plantation owner, these women would often be verbally and physically abused by the jealous plantation mistress.

Brutal beatings with cat-o-nine-tails that ripped the flesh off the bone could be given for a number of reasons. These included praying for freedom, wearing the wrong facial expression, eating without permission, reading a book, holding a book, and plantation owners experiencing mood swings.

The plantation experience was filled with a high level of physical violence and the threat of the same. Therefore, many African slaves lived on the brink of emotional and psychological breakdown.

MATERIAL DEPRIVATION

Unlike the system of Jim Crow/legal segregation, the plantation system brought White plantation owners and enslaved Africans in close contact with one another. Plantation owners were constrained to know as much as possible about enslaved Africans in order to maintain maximal control over them. Enslaved Africans owned little property or materials on the plantation. They lived in squalid conditions, especially those that worked in the fields. Their clothes were tattered, shabby and did not provide adequate protection from the brutal cold of winter or the burning sun of summer.

Enslaved Africans oftentimes were not adequately fed. In *Bullwhip Days*, former slave Louise Adams recounts the food situation. She recalls: "We were so hongry we were bound to steal or perish." Things were much different for many plantation owners. They possessed an abundance of material goods—fine clothes, jewelry, an abundance of food—and they lived in comfortable, sometimes lavish living quarters. The relationship plantation owners structured between themselves and enslaved Africans generated an aching sense of awareness within the enslaved African community of their destitute and inadequate conditions.

Free Africans did not live much better than the enslaved. In some ways the quality of life was worse for them than for their enslaved counterparts. In his book, *Black Labor, White Wealth*, Dr. Claud Anderson writes:

> In the mid-1800s the living conditions for free blacks were so desperate that nearly 50 percent had no choice but to seek some form of public welfare. In order to survive, large numbers of blacks publicly acknowledged that they were in a helpless state and were incapable of feeding, protecting, sheltering and educating themselves and their children. Many black families became so desperate that they voluntarily re-entered slavery to survive. Others turned to public charity.

PSYCHIC VIOLENCE

Enslaved Africans who worked in the masta's house were often light-skinned. These slaves usually were mulattos born out of rape—a common plantation reality. Enslaved Africans who performed field duties were often dark-skinned. This color-structured work arrangement was the deliberate strategy of the plantation owner. One of the main purposes of this strategy was to maintain division among the enslaved classes, and reduce the risk of an uprising. This psychological tactic proved to be good for plantation owners but damaging to enslaved Africans. It produced an assortment of unhealthy feelings and attitudes within the two classes for one another and themselves. These feelings and attitudes entailed pride, jealousy, envy, animosity, distrust, and hatred. They crippled interpersonal and social relationships amongst the enslaved and created classism within the African community.

The free African population was not exempt from skin color manipulation. It played a major role in determining the degree to which free Africans could participate in the American social system. The system afforded opportunities and privileges to light-skinned free Africans that it did not give dark-skinned ones. The consequence of differing opportunities for light-and dark-skinned free Africans was the creation of a three-tier social structure composed of Whites at the top, light-skinned free Africans in the middle, and dark-skinned free Africans on the bottom.

Skin color had debilitating effects on African American interpersonal relationships. Churches and Greek organizations prohibited dark-skinned Blacks from joining. Some Black families forbade marriage with someone of dark skin. Skin color even incited problems in the Black protest movement. During the revolutionary '60s, light-skinned Black activists were sometimes ostracized by dark-skinned Black activists because they were considered not truly oppressed.

Rewarding light-skinned Blacks with special privileges and opportunities and punishing dark-skinned Blacks with more strenuous work and fewer opportunities produced animosity for being Black, particularly dark-skinned. The cosmetics industry makes billions of dollars because many African Americans hate some of their physical features. Skin color manipulation damaged the Black self-image and created a desire within many Blacks to be White. This positioned Blacks on a slippery psychopathological path of self-destruction.

Studies underscore the fact that dark skin is devalued by many people. Light-skinned Blacks receive greater opportunities than dark-skinned Blacks. The devaluation of dark skin may explain why there are seemingly more dark-skinned Blacks in jail and prison than light.

The following speech was delivered in Virginia in 1712 by a British slave owner from the West Indies named Willie Lynch. It exemplifies the willful, calculated and well-planned attempts by plantation owners to control enslaved Africans through psycho-manipulative strategies and tactics, i.e., skin color manipulation.

Gentlemen: I greet you here on the bank of the James River in the year of Our Lord one thousand seven hundred and twelve. First, I shall thank you The Gentlemen of the Colony of Virginia for bringing me here. I am here to help you solve some of your problems with slaves. Your invitation reached me on my modest plantation in the West Indies where I have experimented with some of the newest and still oldest methods for control of slaves. Ancient Rome would envy us if my program is implemented. As our boat sailed south on the James River, named for our illustrious King, whose version of the Bible we cherish, I saw enough to know that your problem is not elite. White Rome used cords of wood as crosses for standing human bodies along its own highways in great numbers, you are here using the tree and the rope on occasion.

I caught the whiff of a dead slave hanging from a tree a couple miles back. You are not only losing valuable stock by hangings, you are having uprisings, slaves are running away, your crops are sometimes left in the field too long for maximum profit, you suffer occasional fires, your animals are killed, gentlemen, you know what your problems are; I do not need to elaborate. I am not here to enumerate your problems, I am here to introduce you to a method of solving them.

In my bag here, I have a fool proof method for controlling black Slaves. I guarantee everyone of you that if installed correctly it will control the slaves for at least 300 years. My method is simple and members of your family and any Overseer can use it.

I have outlined a number of difference(s) among the slaves; and I take these differences and make them bigger. I use fear, distrust, and envy for control purposes. These methods have worked on my modest plantation in the West Indies and [they] will work throughout the South. Take this simple little list of differences, think about them. On top of my list is "Age" but it is there only because it begins with "A." The second is "Color" or "Shade," there is intelligence, size, sex, size of plantation, status of plantation, attitude of owner, whether the slaves live in the valley, on a hill, East, West, North, or South, have a fine or course hair, or is tall or short. Now that you have a list of differences, I shall give you an outline of action but before that, I shall assure you that distrust is stronger than trust and envy is stronger than adulation, respect and admiration. The black Slave, after receiving this indoctrination, shall carry on and will become self-refueling and self-generating for hundreds of years, maybe thousands.

Don't forget you must pitch the old black versus the young black and the young black male against the old black male. You must use the dark skin slave vs. the light skin slaves and the light skin slaves vs. the dark skin slaves. You must also have your white servants and overseer distrust all blacks, but it is necessary that your slaves trust and depend on us. They must love, respect and trust only us.

Gentlemen, these kits are keys to control, use them. Have your wives and children use them, never miss an opportunity. My plan is guaranteed and the good thing about this plan is that if used intensely for one year the slaves themselves will remain perpetually distrustful.

Thank you, gentlemen.

POST-SLAVERY PHASE
PHYSICAL VIOLENCE

The abolishment of chattel slavery gave birth to a cruel and inhumane system of Black/White separation known as Jim Crow. The Jim Crow era was a humiliating and physically brutal time for Blacks. While the Thirteenth Amendment provided Blacks statutory freedom, it did not protect them from the tidal wave of racist brutality that was ushered in with the ushering out of Reconstruction.

The Ku Klux Klan emerged in May of 1865. Their mission was to protect White Southerners from White Northern political philosophies, and from Blacks everywhere[8]. Lynch mob attacks were a bitter reality during the early Jim Crow era, particularly in the South. These gangs were largely responsible for the lynching of more than 2,500 Blacks between 1880 and 1900. Between 1900 and the beginning of World War I, the number of Black lynchings had climbed to more than 4,000[9]. Blacks were hung, shot and burned alive at the stake. The summer of 1919, which is known as "Red Summer," was filled with the violent attack and murder of Blacks. It was called Red Summer because the blood of Black folk poured into the streets.

The murder of Sam Holt by a Florida lynch mob, as told by a Kissimmee Valley Gazette reporter, is a searing example of the sadistic acts of violence Whites perpetrated against guilty and innocent Blacks. Below are excerpts from that newspaper article.

"SAM HOLT BURNED AT STAKE"
APRIL 28, 1899

Sam Holt, the negro who is thought to have murdered Alfred Cranford and assailed Cranford's wife, was burned at the stake one mile and a quarter from Newnan, Ga., Sunday afternoon, July 23rd, at 2:30 o'clock. Fully 2,000 people surrounded the small sapling to which he was fastened and watched the flames eat away his flesh, saw his body mutilated by knives and witnessed the contortions of his body in his extreme agony.

For sickening sights, harrowing details and blood-curdling incidents, the burning of Holt is unsurpassed by any occurrence of a like kind ever heard in the history of Georgia. A few smoldering ashes scattered about the place, a blackened stake, are all that was left to tell the story.

Holt went to the stake with as much courage as anyone could possibly have possessed on such an occasion, and the only murmur that issued from his lips was when angry knives plunged into his flesh and his life's blood sizzled in the fire before his eyes.

Masks played no part of the lynching. There was no secrecy; no effort to prevent anyone seeing who lighted the fire, who cut off the ears or who took the head. On the trunk of a tree nearby was pinned the following placard: "We Must Protect Our Southern Women[10]."

In October 1929, the stock market plunged, hurling the country into the Great Depression. Whites took their hard economic times out on Blacks through perpetrating cruel acts of violence against them. Blacks again became regular victims of arbitrary Ku Klux Klan and lynch mob gang terrorization, beatings and lynchings.

The Civil Rights Movement roused White anxiety. Between the 1950s and 1960s racially motivated street riots were common. Whites rioted through the criminal justice system as well. Blacks were spied on by the military and police. Black men, women, boys and girls were beaten in the streets by police, attacked with water hoses and vicious dogs and even murdered. Black life in America was consumed with White violence.

What effect did being consumed with degrading violence have on African Americans? Enslaved Africans became spiteful of plantation owners and their property. The enslaved Africans' perceived lack of power often prevented them from attacking plantation owners outright. Consequently, they attacked the next best thing—the owners' property. Even today the commission of property crimes is viewed by many Black offenders as "taking from the White man." This perverted logic is traceable to the plantation experience.

These experiences evoked a deep resentment within many Blacks for being Black. They blamed their oppression on their Blackness. A steady stream of Black self-hatred flows out of this attitude. Black self-hatred is not a new phenomenon. The seeds of Black self-hatred were sown in the minds of Blacks at the time of European invasion and it continues to grow.

Black self-hatred is a psychopathology that develops because Blacks internalize White racism. It motivates them to think and act like a White racist. They disrespect themselves and other Blacks. This is demonstrated in calling themselves and other Blacks "nigga" and "bitch." It generates the highest forms of disrespect for self, "Black-on-Black" murder and Black suicide. Black self-hatred prohibits Blacks from seeing the social root cause

43

of their oppressive conditions—White racism.

LAW ENFORCEMENT'S ASSAULT ON
BLACK LEADERSHIP AND ORGANIZATION

Since systemized law enforcement was established in America more than 150 years ago, it has been used by the ruling elite to keep African Americans under control. The police maintained control through surveillance, terrorization, criminalization and extermination. The system of law enforcement has also served as an instigator of disruption in Black protest organizations. Structured law enforcement brought a sense of legitimacy, righteousness and authority to the attack on Black protest organizations and its front-line leadership.

When the Federal Bureau of Investigation was organized in the early 1900s, one of its more important responsibilities was to harass and intimidate Black leaders, maintain surveillance on Black protest organizations and bring them to their demise. The destruction of the Marcus Garvey movement of the 1920s was one of the Federal Bureau Investigation's first major victories against Black protest in America. However, the most sophisticated and sinister attack—that we know of—on Black protest in America was done by the Counter Intelligence Program, a.k.a. COINTELPRO.

COINTELPRO is discussed in greater detail in a later essay; therefore, limited time will be spent on this subject. COINTELPRO was initially designed to frustrate the Communist Party U.S.A. movement. However, it evolved into an operation that unmercifully assaulted the Black protest movement. It utilized an array of extra-legal and deceptive tactics that included sending fraudulent letters to Black organizations to incite animosity between Black leaders, planting informants, conducting surveillance on Black leaders, manipulating the media and legal establishments, and the murder of Black leaders[11]. COINTELPRO frustrated the Black protest movement. It engineered social disorder and disorganization. It created high levels of Black unrest. The effects of COINTELPRO were underpinnings that took "Black-on-Black" crime and violence to higher levels.

UNITED STATES GOVERNMENT PLOT TO
IMMOBILIZE GLOBAL AFRICAN RELATIONS

In his book, *Success Runs In Our Race*, George Fraser provides information that reveals that tactics used to control enslaved Africans have been modified for usage on the contemporary African American and Black African communities. Fraser writes:

> Interestingly on March 17, 1978, a secret memorandum was issued to the president and his Cabinet as part of a "comprehensive review

of current developments in black Africa from the point of view of their possible impacts on the black movement in the United States." It was an analysis of the strategic social, economic, and political ramifications made by then-chairman of the National Security Council Zbigniew Brzezinski under Jimmy Carter.

He later wrote:

It was Brzezinski's position at the time that it was not in the best interest of the U.S. to allow any part of the U.S. black movement to show outreach and support of the emerging movement in black Africa.

A "range of policy options" were listed in this memo. I wish to make note of three of them.

to elaborate and bring in to effect a special program designed to perpetuate division in the black movement to neutralize the most active groups of leftist radical organizations representing different social strata of the black community to encourage divisions in black circles.

to work out and realize preventative operations in order to impede durable ties between U.S. black organizations and radical groups in African states.

to support actions designed to sharpen social stratification in the black community which would lead to the widening and perpetuation of the gap between successful educated blacks and the poor, giving rise to growing antagonism between different black groups and weakening of the movement as a whole.

PSYCHIC VIOLENCE I

American culture is centered on Europe and people of European descent. Europeans offer themselves as standards of all things good and excellent, i.e., intelligence, beauty, art, etc. White Americans reduced Blacks to the level of three-fifths human under the law. Black men were called boys and Black women were called girls. Scientists declared that Blacks were inherently inferior to Whites. Blacks were forbidden to look Whites directly in their eyes. Every facet of Jim Crow/legal segregation spoke of Black America's inferior position in America.

Even today the very character of Black people is attacked in America. The media portray Blacks as inferior to Whites, criminals, sexual gluttons, clowns and social dependents. These images contaminate Black self-image and self-concept. They are dynamics that inflict bruises, scars and lacerations on the Black psyche.

Many Blacks struggle to climb out of poverty. They are consigned to crowded, substandard living conditions. The educational system resists African centered education. It places disproportionately high numbers of Blacks in special education classes. Moreover, they suspend disproportionately high numbers of Blacks. The African American experience has been one of enduring continuous blows to the psyche. This psychic wounding and contamination produces a psychological disease called *inferiorization*. In *The Isis Papers*, Dr. Welsing defines inferiorization:

> Inferiorization is the conscious, deliberate and systematic process utilized specifically by a racist (white supremacy) social system, as conducted through all of its major and minor institutions (including the institution of family), to mold specific peoples within that system (namely, all peoples classified by the racist system as non-white) into "functional inferiors," in spite of their true genetic potential for functioning.

The intellectual potential and artistic talents of Black people are stymied in America—certain athletic, singing and acting talents excluded. African Americans must recognize that they live in a social system which wastes its potential. It must design strategies to counter this psychologically violent social process and realize the maximal development of the collective Black community.

PSYCHIC VIOLENCE II

The level of media saturation in America today has never been greater in media history. Therefore, the risk of being psychologically harmed by the power of the media has never been greater. There are many items on the mass media menu. They include radio, television, billboards, motion pictures, books, magazines, newspapers, newsletters, flyers, etc. Every form of media possesses tremendous potential to influence the human personality. However, the forms of media that have both visual and audio capabilities possess the greatest potential of influence. Television and motion pictures possess both those capabilities.

Hundreds of studies have been conducted to determine the influence television has on viewers. The Center for Research on the Influence of Television on Children has produced information that suggests that television does in fact have damaging affects on children. Their studies have revealed that children who watch violent programing tend to exhibit more aggressive behavior than children who do not.

Nielson figures report that the average African American watches 77.3 hours of television per week. This amounts to more than 4,000 hours of television viewing per year. By age 16, the "average youth" has watched 200,000 acts of violence and 33,000 murders on television. Since African Americans watch more than the average amount of television, the numbers are higher for them.

African American children identify closely with characters they see on television, particularly Black characters. These characters also serve as role model sources for Black children. The tragedy is television often depicts African Americans in inferior roles. Michigan State University conducted a study of Black children and television in 1978. It found that:

- Black children believed that television was true to life.
- Forty-five percent of elementary school children believed that blacks on television were representative of blacks in real life.
- Commercials are more believable for black children than white children.
- Over 50 percent of all black children between the ages of 5 and 12 believe that commercials present true and accurate information.

Motion pictures have been slandering and distorting the Black image for more than a century. This section will concentrate only on the last quarter century of motion picture history in America. The early '70s marked a period in American cinematic history where the Black image and the Black psyche would suffer significant damage. It was called the Blaxploitation Era[12].

Three movies launched the motion picture industry into this era. These movies were *Sweet Sweetback's Baadasssss Song* produced by Melvin Van Peebles (1971), *Shaft* produced by Gordon Parks, Sr. (1971), and *Superfly* produced by Gordon Parks, Jr. (1972). The success of these pioneering films motivated movie makers to produce a host of motion pictures after their order. Some of these movies included *T.N.T., The Legend of Nigger Charley, The Soul of Nigger Charley, Cleopatra Jones, Willie Dynamite, Book of Numbers, Black Caesar, Hell Up in Harlem, Foxy Brown, J.D.'s Revenge, Slaughter, Slaughter's Big Rip Off,* etc[13]. By the late '70s, the coffin was closing on Blaxploitation flicks.

In 1985, a predominantly Black cast appeared on the silver screen in a movie produced by Steven Speilberg called, *The Color Purple. The Color Purple* was taken from Alice Walker's book with the same title. This motion picture essentially was about an uncomely Black girl named Celie, played by Whoopie Goldberg, who is molested by her stepfather and gets pregnant. She is later forced to marry an abusive Black man named Mister, played by Danny Glover. Celie's relationship with her husband's love interest, Shug, with whom she experiences a lesbian encounter, sparks her awakening that leads to her leaving her husband. This motion picture received a great deal of praise by Whites and Blacks despite the projection of negative images of Black men and women.

Black cinematic culture received a much needed jolt with the 1985 release of Spike Lee's *She's Gotta Have It*. Spike went on to produce *Do The Right Thing*, *Jungle Fever*, *Mo' Better Blues* and *Malcolm X*. His work is not loved by all Blacks. However, Spike has produced movies that portray Blacks in cognition rather than the usual exotic roles such as hustlers, prostitutes, drug dealers and drive-by shooters. However, in March, 1991, just when Spike was "doing the right thing," Nino Brown, the New Jack Hustler was introduced to America in *New Jack City* directed by Mario Van Peebles. *New Jack City* resurrected Blaxploitation cinema, which incidentally Mario's father, Melvin Van Peebles, helped pioneer. This movie certainly was an ingenious production, and Wesley Snipes did give an outstanding performance. However, this film did nothing more than give drug dealers grand ideas, reaffirm criminal stereotypes of Black people, romanticize Black crime and further damage the Black image.

The success of *New Jack City* paved the way for a number of ghetto dramas to grace the big screen. They include *Colors*, *Juice*, *Boyz N The Hood*, *Trespass*, *Strapped* (HBO), *Menace II Society*, *Sugar Hill*, *New Jersey Drive*, *Clockers*, *Dead Presidents* and others. These movies starred attractive and charismatic Black men and women who demonstrated impressive acting abilities. Lorenz Tate's performance in Allen and Albert Hughes' ghetto thriller, *Menace II Society*, was particularly impressive. Tate's portrayal of a psychopathic young brother in South Central Los Angeles named O-Dog mesmerized audiences. He was particularly compelling in the scene where he, Awax and Cain were on their way to "smoke" those fellas' that "popped" Cain, and did a "1-8-7" on his cousin in a car-jacking.

The primary problem with ghetto thrillers is image. African Americans are seen in singular dimension. These movies make it tempting to view African American communities as places devoured by gun totin', 40 sippin', gang bangin', psychopathic, crack slangin', coke sniffin' Blacks.

The strong criminal image these movies project presents a serious problem with youth. Youth are emulators, particularly young males. Shortly after *Menace II Society* was released, three young Black males in my hometown, Fort Worth, Texas, walked into an Asian-owned convenience store and committed robbery and murder. *Menace II Society* opens with Cain and O-Dog walking into an Asian-owned convience store to buy some beer. This visit climaxes with O-Dog shooting the Asian man and woman several times, killing them and taking a wad of money.

The brain-computer of youths is delicate and highly impressionable. Sometimes even when parenting is sufficient, the strong appeal of certain negative social variables can overshadow a parent's healthy influence. This is why the whole village should be involved in rearing children, including movie makers and entertainers. While many teenagers talk, dress and have the body of an adult, they are not psychologically and emotionally mature.

These movies may close by sending a dynamic positive message, but that message, which lasts maybe five minutes, is often undercut by the two hours of dynamic profanity, sex, drugs, misogyny and violence sugar-coated with glamor.

Another variable that beats on the mind of our youth is music videos. The blend of graphic images, hypnotic beats and provocative lyrics is a dangerous formula for psychological disorder. Most gangsta rap videos, whether they intend to or not, exalt and celebrate the dangerous lifestyle of gangsterism. By associating crime and violence with admired artists, they acquire an alluring appeal to young people, especially those who suffer in their identity and self-image.

Gangsta rap songs and videos inspire a lifestyle that directly opposes Black liberation. They generally reinforce self-hate, devalue genuine brotherhood, underrate intellectual excellence, and create the feeling that the negative realities of the ghetto can not be changed. Gangsta rappers argue that their videos speak to the reality of the ghetto. The truth is they speak to only one reality of the ghetto. Most inner-city African Americans are hard-working, law-abiding people, they are not criminals.

Four

Post-Segregation Black Parents: Unwitting Agents of the Seduction?

One way the legacy of European oppression of Black people manifests itself is through disrupted Black social institutions. The plight of Blacks in America is to a great degree the consequence of their inability to extinguish the destructive power of White racism due to serious breakdowns and collapses within their social institutions. The breakdown of Black social institutions was no accident. It was prescribed by the ruling elite in order that they may manage Blacks and retain control of America's political-economic systems. The repair and rebuilding of Black social institutions should be the principal objective of Blacks in America. In fact, it would be wise for Blacks to consider whether some of their institutions should be torn down and rebuilt entirely.

Black leadership in America has failed to cultivate new leadership. This has prohibited the development of more diversified approaches to solving Black problems. Heretofore, one of the main strategies employed to advance Blacks in America was negotiating and bargaining. Maximal progress cannot be achieved by relying too heavily on these strategies. Powerful people will never negotiate away their power to the powerless; the powerless must take it. And this power must be taken through employing a diversity of proactive and reactive strategic activities.

As long as Black social institutions remain in the throes of disruption and disorder, their focus will largely be on survival, and their ability to be strategically diversified will be greatly reduced. In fact, as long as Black social institutions remain broken, the power that Blacks possess will continually be depleted, because its brokenness permits Whites and others to exploit and disempower them.

It is incumbent upon Blacks in America to place the building of sound and stable institutions on the top of their agenda. These institutions include religion, education, economics, labor, health, entertainment, politics, justice, leadership and family.

PEOPLE SELF-DESTRUCT FOR LACK OF KNOWLEDGE

African Americans must understand that racism/White supremacy is a major cause of many Black problems. This understanding is crucial for many reasons. The thorough knowledge of Black oppression helps resolve Black self-hatred. An inept understanding of oppression will cause the oppressed group to blame themselves for their conditions.

The inept understanding of Black oppression eliminates a huge variable that contributes to the Black plight. When the variable of Black oppression is eliminated, Blacks are left with few variables to consider when they are determining causes to their problems. Consequently, Blacks become uppermost in their minds as causes to their problems. When Blacks think that they are the sole cause to their problems, they consciously or subconsciously hate themselves for being Black. The full understanding of the legacy of Black oppression helps resolve Black self-hatred, because Blacks are then able to realize that their problems are not the consequence of being Black, but of racism in the minds of oppressive Whites.

However, it is likewise vitally important that African Americans possess a thorough understanding of how they contribute to the perpetuation of their problems. Self-evaluation can be difficult and even painful, but without this understanding the eradication of racism/White supremacy would not guarantee an end to the plight of Black people in America. This essay boldly looks at the institution of the African American family, namely parents, and considers the ways in which they contribute to the perpetuation of crime and violence in the African American community.

AFRICAN FAMILY DISORDER: A REQUIREMENT FOR WHITE DOMINATION

The foundation of African American culture is the African American family unit, in particular the parental component, and the African American church. The African American church is actually an "expanded Black family." The church depends on the family for strength just as the family depends on it for strength. The value of church involvement is largely instilled into children by their parents. Clearly, Africans in America would not have survived the Maafa as well as they did without supportive and courageous parents.

Unfortunately, many Black parents have been enlisted into the seduction machination. These parents are "unwitting agents of the seduction." They qualify as unwitting agents because they possess inept child development skills and an inability to meet the strenuous psychological and emotional demands of parenting.

Africans enjoyed healthy and progressive civilizations prior to the European invasion. African civilizations, though not perfect, served as standards for other cultures in the world. African enslavement however, contaminated African culture and values. This was key to the successful operation of the American slave institution. Whites exercised a variety of tactics to disrupt the African family unit. Among them—swift and abrupt family separation, the abolishment of marriage, stripping males of family responsibilities, prohibiting bonding between parents and children, and weakening parental roles, particularly the role of the father. African American oppression did not ravage the African family unit, but it did leave indelible marks carved on parents, which can be seen in their child rearing styles and techniques.

TWO UNWITTING AGENTS

It requires a tremendous amount of courage and maturity to engage in self-criticism for the purpose of pinpointing one's flaws and deficiencies. African American parents must build the courage to access their parenting styles and techniques to determine which techniques need enhancement or to be totally discarded. The African American family will not develop and become a stabilized unit if parents fail to be self-critical.

There are many examples of adequate parental models in the African American community. However, there are far too many examples of deficient parents. My personal observation of Black parents on a day-to-day basis, and as a law officer, coupled with analytical study of them revealed two major types of inadequate Black parents. They include "double-minded parents" and "teenage parents."

DOUBLE-MINDED PARENTS

The maintenance of the American slave institution made the contamination of African culture a necessity. A rich and intact culture strengthens and edifies a people. The success of American slavery hinged upon the enslaved possessing weak minds which discouraged resistance of gross exploitation, and robust bodies to perform strenuous work in the plantation system. The richness of African culture produced people who achieved high levels of thinking, experienced unity, and sound relationships. Had African culture not been contaminated, enslaved Africans would have worked harder in the fields of resistance than the fields of cotton.

Africans were thrust into a culture that was diametrically opposed to theirs. The consequence of being thrust into a foreign culture, which they were not permitted to fully participate in, and having their culture contaminated was the creation of a "split culture." In *The Developmental Psychology of the Black Child*, Dr. Amos Wilson underscores this belief by commenting:

> Black people in America do not belong to any one functional, coherent, cohesive culture. They belong to neither the white culture nor to one they can call their own. Culturally speaking, blacks exist between "the devil" of the dominant white world to which he is not permitted to fully belong, and "the deep blue sea" of the current dysfunctional black world to which he also is not permitted to belong.

The disjointed nature of life in America for Blacks pounds on their personality and consciousness. This experience can be compared to that of an undercover agent. By day, the agent assimilates into a life of corruption posing as a delinquent student, a drug addict or a drug dealer. By night, he sheds his false identity and tries to resume a normal lifestyle. The psychological strain of maintaining dual personalities simultaneously over an extended period of time has caused many agents to developed deep emotional and psychological problems that lead to drug and alcohol abuse. Sometimes the problems become so acute that long-term professional intervention is needed.

I am aware of the mental effect of maintaining dual personalities over a long period of time. For nearly fifteen months I worked as an undercover narcotic officer. Six of those months were spent portraying a student at a high school in the city where I reside. I experienced a high degree of emotional and psychological pressure from the strain of suppressing my true identity, and the fear that one day I would be discovered. This job affected certain areas of my personal life as well.

The divided nature of life in America for Blacks can have similar emotional and psychological affects on them. Blacks in America live under persistent pressure to be bicultural. In order to survive they must abide by the codes of White and Black culture. Differences in the experiences of Blacks and Whites in world history create physical and psychological differences between the two groups. For instance, hair texture, skin color and facial features of Blacks and Whites are different because their historical experiences are different.

Insecurity causes many Whites to be uncomfortable with differences between themselves and Blacks. This insecurity is manifest when Whites demean the dark skin and other physical features of Blacks, while at the same time having cosmetic surgery and baking themselves in the sun to acquire the very characteristics they demean. Although Whites have prohibited the creation of Black culture, they do not want Blacks to fully enter into theirs. Consequently, Blacks experience what Dr. W.E.B. Dubois referred to as "Double Consciousness." In *The Souls of Black Folks*, Dubois wrote:

> The Negro is a sort of seventh son born with a veil, and gifted with second sight in this American world—a world which yields him no true self-consciousness, but only lets him see himself through the eyes of others, of measuring one's soul by the tape of a world that looks on in amused contempt and pity. One ever feels his two-ness— an American, a Negro; two souls, two thoughts, two unreconciled strivings; two warring ideals in one black body, whose dogged strength alone keeps it from being torn asunder.
>
> The history of the American Negro is the history of this strife— this longing to attain self-conscious manhood, to merge his double self into a better and truer self. In this merging he wishes neither of the older selves to be lost. He would not Africanize America, for America has too much to teach the world and Africa. He would not bleach his Negro soul in a flood of white Americanism, for he knows that Negro blood has a message for the world. He simply wishes to make it possible for a man to be both a Negro and an American, without being cursed and spit upon by his fellows, without having the door of opportunity closed roughly in his face.

A Black person in America who decides to commit to African culture will be perceived as "radical." Such a decision can be costly. The dominant White American culture punishes non-Whites, particularly Blacks, who do not conform to its culture. For those who do, it gives "repossessable rewards." However, even conformists experience frustration. Ellis Cose discusses this in his book entitled *The Rage of a Privileged Class*:

> For most blacks in America, regardless of status, political persuasion, or accomplishments, the moment never arrives when race can be treated as a total irrelevancy. Instead, too often it is the only relevant factor defining our existence.

The Black experience in America generates a split personality—one side is White, the other, Black. James 1:8 reads: A double-minded man is unstable in all his ways. The psychological condition of double-mindedness causes the Black person in America to become instable, unbalanced and inconsistent in their thought and behavior. Double-mindedness diminishes a parent's capacity to be stable, balanced and consistent in child rearing. This trio is vital in order for a child to travel safely through the difficult developmental process.

People experiencing double-mindedness can often be recognized by their views on race matters and esthetics (physical beauty), skin color in particular. Skin color created a great deal of friction within the free and enslaved African communities. It remains a contentious matter in contemporary African American culture. By placing light-skinned Blacks above dark-skinned Blacks within the plantation system, the plantation owner generated what Kathy Russell, Midge Wilson and Ronald Hall call The Color Complex, which is also the title of their book. The color complex comprises those subconscious and/or conscious attitudes Blacks possess regarding Black esthetics, which in turn create intra-racial bias and discrimination. The color complex affects dating habits, marital choices, and social and professional opportunities.

Skin color can also have injurious influences on the Black parent/child relationship. The color complex, which only the double-minded person can experience, can cause a parent to discriminate between light- and dark-skinned children. This has debilitating affects on child development. It deprives children of balanced and consistent discipline and nurturing. Without these, Black children can experience feelings of rejection, inferiority and self-hate.

The true story of a young girl I will call Tammy Smith offers a practical demonstration of double-minded parenting and its negative effects on children. Tammy is 14 years old and lives in a Southern city of average size. She lives with her mother Joyce, and her two sisters, Sharon, 15, and Cynthia, 16. Tammy's father is not in the household and does not visit. Tammy's mother allows Sharon and Cynthia to do things Tammy cannot. They can have boyfriends and come and go virtually as they please. However, Tammy is not allowed to have a boyfriend, and she is restricted from participating in many outdoor activities.

Tammy resents her mother for being so unfair to her. She often defies her orders by staying out late at night, and seeing a number of different boys. Joyce never deals with Tammy's rebelliousness in the same manner. Sometimes she physically beats Tammy, other times she finds it amusing and laughs at her.

What distinguishes Tammy from her sisters is her esthetic features. Sharon and Cynthia are light-skinned with long, straight hair. Tammy is dark with short, coarse hair. Her mother and sisters tease her because she is "black" with short, "nappy" hair. Incidentally, Tammy has performed exceptionally well in school. However, over the last two years she has been nothing but trouble for her teachers and administrators. There are many Tammys in America today.

This story demonstrates that esthetics can affect a parent's child rearing practices. Double-minded Black parents like Joyce lack the ability to be consistently stable, balanced and unwavering in the rearing of their children. These parents experience a love/hate relationship with certain children. This co-mingling of opposing emotions and attitudes can cause the parent to be lenient at one time, then suddenly become strict. They may be accepting at one moment, and rejecting the next[14].

Children with dark skin can be treated harshly at times simply because they have dark skin. Dark skin is the mark of oppression. Therefore, it can trigger the deep-seated hatred and resentment double-minded parents hold for dark skin. The double-minded parent may therefore treat the dark child harshly because his dark skin symbolizes bitter pain. Conversely, the double-minded parent may shower the child with material things in an attempt to deflect the pain that is felt by being Black.

Children of double-minded parents are highly susceptible to developing all sorts of personality weaknesses. These weaknesses reduce the Black child's ability to cope with the stress of living in a racist society. As they grow older, they may wrestle with feelings of confusion, insecurity, inferiority and feeling unloved. They may develop a negative self-image and broken self-esteem. They are then highly vulnerable to becoming rebellious, sexually promiscuous, and involved in crime and violence. The child may also resort to using various drugs to medicate themselves and ease the pain they feel.

A Bureau of Justice Statistics report entitled *Young Black Male Victimization* reveals that between 1973 and 1992, the rate of violent victimizations of young Black males increased about 25 percent. Most victims of violence are victimized by someone of their own race. I believe there is a direct relationship between the noticeable increase in violence among Black teenagers during the late '70s and early '80s, and societal circumstances. Blacks who entered their teens during the late '70s and early '80s were born during a period when the nation was making the turbulent transition from segregated to integrated society. Integration brought political and economical opportunities for some Blacks, but psychic pain for most, particularly the youth. Black youth experienced busing, life in racially intolerant White suburbs, and racially motivated harassment.

Moreover, many Black children did not receive adequate psychological, emotional and spiritual nurture from their parents. Integration placed cultural mandates and time restraints on Black parents. The move into mainstream society forced Blacks to focus more on the needs of the larger culture than on their own. They became less passionate about building a strong Black American social and economic system.

Better jobs afforded many Blacks the opportunity to pursue the "American dream." The pursuit of this dream made many Black children have nightmares. Their parents were spending less time with them. Work was not the only thing that robbed Black children of parental attention. The illusive atmosphere of tremendous Black progress generated the "Love and Happiness Era." This was the party era of the early and mid-'70s.

Black people's waning commitment to Black culture and community, their growing commitment to the larger culture, and the pleasures that came with this "better life" shifted Black values from God and family toward thrill seeking and the accumulation of material things. Many Black parents gave their children televisions, personal telephones, cars, clothes and freedoms in place of love, affection, attention and consistent discipline. Many Black parents figured if they gave their children all the *things* they did not get while growing up during Jim Crow, their children would become better people.

Black parents also began warehousing their children in daycare centers and leaving them home alone in order to amass the material things to give them. Many Black parents, particularly single Black parents, had to work extra jobs in order to make ends meet. This is because integration took many of the good paying jobs out of the urban Black community.

The Black community is currently paying dearly for its double-mindedness. It sowed the wind in the late '60s and early '70s, and began reaping the whirlwind in the '80s. Many Black children who did not receive adequate amounts of love, attention and acceptance from parents sought them in the streets. However, they did not find genuine love. They found a perverted version of parental love, attention and acceptance called gang love, and they found a sex partner. Consequently, the numbers of teenage parents in the Black community increased sharply during the '70s and '80s. They are the second unwitting agent of the seduction.

TEENAGE BLACK PARENTS

Blacks yearned to assimilate with Whites because they felt it would greatly improve their lives. They felt Black education would improve if Black children were schooled in White classrooms, Black economics would be strengthened by working in mainstream jobs, and their lives would be enhanced by living in White suburbs.

The collective Black community has seen many things improve since integration. However, the Black community has regressed in many ways. Integration facilitated the breakdown of Black social institutions. It contaminated Black values, particularly family values. Many Black parents spent less time with their children. This meant less time holding, cuddling and talking to their children. They were busy working long hours to survive, engaged in conspicuous consumption, or they were partying. This value shift took its toll on the emotional and psychological health of Black children. Sexual promiscuity became a substitute for parental love. Consequently, the numbers of young Black females giving birth to children began rising in the late '70s. Observe these startling statistics reported in an article contained in the National Urban League's State of Black America Report 1989 entitled *Black Children in America*:

- Each day in 1986, 1,702 infants were born to black women of all ages.
- Almost one in four was born to a teenager.
- 1,042 were born to unmarried mothers.
- 450 were born to mothers with less than a high school education.

Each day in 1986, about 700 black girls between the ages of 15 and 19 became pregnant, and an estimated 250 had abortions.

- Nine in ten were born to unmarried teens.
- One in four was born to a teenage mother with at least one other child.
- Sixteen were born to mothers younger than age fifteen.

In an essay contained in *The Isis Papers* entitled *Black Child-Parents: The New Factor in Black Genocide*, Welsing writes:

> If present conditions persist [25 percent of Black children being born to Black teenagers], history will record that Black people living in the U.S. failed to survive the 20th century A.D. This failure will occur, not simply because they were a captured and oppressed people, but because they permitted themselves to become a blind people without any social vision or understanding. History may record that Black elders, fathers, mothers had no vision, and therefore the Black children became stupid, thinking that they could nurture something as precious as the life of a new human being. As a result of all this, Black people perished.

Being a parent is a tremendously awesome responsibility. It demands from an individual high levels of emotional and psychological functioning. The work of parenting produces its best results in children when fully mature mothers and fathers, or models thereof, participate in the child-rearing process. Teenagers are not capable of performing on the high levels of emotional and psychological maturity necessary for effective parenting. They cannot maintain male/female relationships so that both parents can participate in child rearing through the entire process. Although rare exceptions exist, teenagers do not make adequate parents.

Teenagers have to graduate through several levels of maturity before they reach a place in development where they would make adequate parents.

Even mature parents are challenged by the strains and demands of parenting. These strains and demands cause immature parents, such as teenagers, to plunge to deeper levels of immaturity. They neutralize the maturation process and send them into an emotional and psychological backsliding process.

Money and time are necessary to be adequate parents. Teenagers are challenged by their demands. They become easily distracted by "youthful activities." They often depend on their parents and other relatives for financial support. This places great strain on their already inadequate emotional and psychological resources. This strain renders them incapable of providing their child with the stable and nurturing environment they need to move safely through the developmental process. One of the supreme challenges of successful parenting is its demand for consistency. To achieve maximal child development, the parent must parent consistently through every stage of child development. This process is more than two decades long!

Because teenage parents do not possess an adequate amount of emotional and psychological maturity, they become fatigued. Fatigue then leads to resentment, resentment leads to rejection and rejection leads to neglect. Children react in a variety of unhealthy ways when their legitimate needs are not met. These reactions may include the need for constant attention, bed wetting, eating disorders, excessive displays of temper tantrums, crying fits, stubbornness, rebelliousness, etc. As the child approaches adolescence, the pain of parental neglect manifests itself through a driving desire to block that pain with drugs and alcohol, involvement in crime and violence, and the pursuit of love through sex. The deadly cycle continues.

INTEGRATION AND THE DISINTEGRATION OF THE URBAN BLACK COMMUNITY SET THE STAGE FOR THE VIOLENT DRAMA

Integration set the stage for the frightening drama of crime and violence in the African American community. It motivated the exodus of the Black middle class from the urban Black community into the suburbs. Prior to integration, conditions in urban Black communities overall were fairly stable, considering the oppressive circumstances. However, the middle class Black flight took away the urban Black community's defenses. It had no buffers to absorb the blows of racism; hence it felt the full brunt of oppression.

The exodus of the Black middle class took away successful models of family, educational achievement and business. Legal segregation had pressed Blacks of virtually every socioeconomic level into relating with one another. Doctors lived next to maids, lawyers lived next to corner store owners, teachers lived next to sanitation workers, etc. Black communities lived by the principle of collective work and responsibility.

During this era, Black people felt that it was their responsibility to ensure that the neighborhood children made a safe transition into adulthood. This created an extended family network that permitted constant supervision over neighborhood children and their discipline when it was needed.

Integration robbed urban Black communities of stabilizing capital. The flight of the Black middle class left communities filled with jobless poor and working poor. Consequently, Black businesses such as banks, restaurants, grocery stores and gas stations failed.

Blacks lost control of the classroom with integration. Black teachers lost jobs, Black principals were demoted, Black schools were closed, and White educators who had no experience in dealing with Black children began teaching and miseducating Black children.

The flight of the Black middle class who were the models of success, the weakening of the collective work principle, the loss of stabilizing capital, the near demise of urban Black enterprise, and incompetent education sent urban Black communities plummeting into deterioration. The resulting frustration and stress turned the wheels of an urban "Black-on-Black" cycle of violence.

FIVE

THE PSYCHOLOGY OF GANGSTERISM:
IT EXISTED LONG BEFORE MONSTER KODY

Violence is as American as Cherry Pie.
H. Rap Brown

Black people arrest White people's attention in two ways, as exotic objects, such as athletes and entertainers, or transgressive creatures, such as violent criminals and political revolutionaries. Sanyika Shakur, a.k.a. Monster Kody Scott, captured America's attention for a short period in 1994 as the transgressive creature. Formerly a key member of a South Central Los Angeles gang, Sanyika highlighted his gang exploits in a highly controversial book entitled *MONSTER*. This book turned the national media spotlight on Sanyika. He was a sizzling topic on *60 Minutes*. He was featured on a *Discovery Channel* documentary. A host of articles were written about him in publications throughout the country, and he was also featured in a book about Los Angeles gang culture entitled *Do or Die*.

Sanyika became more than a momentary celebrity—he became a symbol. He became White America's epitome of the American crime problem. When Sanyika appeared on *60 Minutes*, he confirmed the various false perceptions burned in the White mind through media images, crime reports, and other unreliable sources. Sanyika confirmed to Whites that the most serious crime in America is **Black**. His "monstrous" behavior amazed them. While Sanyika's violent actions were grotesque, his acts are a milli-drop in the ocean of America's 400-year legacy of violence. Monster Kody did not deserve the designation of America's supreme violent criminal. Although his violent exploits were abhorrent and unjustifiable, talking about Monster and other "Black bangers" as though they are trend setters of violence is delusionary.

America judges Black crime differently than White crime, for instance. If a group of White surfers in Venice Beach got drunk, destroyed other peoples' property, and raped a young White woman, they would generally be viewed as a group of "misdirected youth" or something similar. However, if some Black youths in Watts got drunk, tagged a building, and raped a young White woman, they would be viewed a gang of thugs.

Mainstream media are guilty of applying double standards in their coverage of crime in America. In his book, *The Mugging of Black America*, Earl Hutchinson shares the results of a study he conducted on the media's coverage of Black versus White crime. It revealed that Black neighborhoods were characterized as drug turfs, war zones, drug infested neighborhoods, urban jungles. Black criminals were described as ghetto outcasts, drug zombies and crime prone. In *Unreliable Sources*, Lee Martin notes that Black criminals have been called mutants, wolves and savages. These negative descriptions are seldom used to describe White neighborhoods, suspects or offenders.

THE GENESIS OF GANGSTERISM IN AMERICA

Psychologists refer to the psychodynamic of gangsterism as a *psychopathology*. This term literally means mental illness. For purposes of this book, gangsterism is defined as:

> a system of exploitation, thievery and perpetrating violence, psychic and/or physical, upon others for the express purpose of an individual or a group satisfying their needs or insatiable desires.

Where does the psychopathology of gangsterism in America originate? The 25-and-under crowd probably surmise that young Black males in South Central L.A. pioneered gangsterism in America. The 35-and-above crowd probably surmise that people such as Al Capone, Baby Face Nelson and John Dillinger are the "fathers of gangsterism." However, did the Crips or Bloods swindle North American territory from Native Americans? Did Al Capone exterminate more than 250,000 Native Americans within a 50-year stretch? Did Baby Face Nelson kidnap and murder millions of Africans in the Middle Passage? Did John Dillinger reduce millions of Africans to animal-like creatures?

It was Christopher Columbus who established the tradition of slaughtering non-Whites in North America. European slave traders murdered millions of Africans. White settlers came to the "New World" with the

Bible in one hand and an indentured servant in the other. White plantation owners exploited millions of Africans and murdered scores of them to ensure their continued exploitation. Christopher Columbus is the "father of gangsterism," and White slave traders, settlers and plantation owners are the "Original Gangsters."

The psychology of gangsterism was a deadly psychodynamic in America long before Monster and the crips and bloods were born. No race in America beats Whites either in the number of crimes and acts of violence committed or the level of egregiousness.

America is obsessed with the exotic nature of violent Black criminals. Young Black males dressed down in red or blue clothing with thin braids in their hair and tattoos about their body seem to titillate the American mind. They are seen on almost all the talk shows, movies are made about them, BET and MTV show videos that celebrate them, and the health and science establishments are engaged in studying them. People act as though this kind of violence is brand new to the American frontier. Black gangsterism, however, did not cause America to "lose her virginity to violence." Black gangsterism is the manifestation of another phase of America's continuing legacy of violence. It is the offspring of the psychopathology of racism.

Listed below are 13 characteristics of Black gangsterism. They permit us to see the striking similarities Black gangsterism and White racism share.

- They associate manhood and masculinity with aggression and violence. Therefore, they use aggression and violence to achieve manhood and to force the respect of others.

- Because they associate manhood with violence, they achieve a perverted sense of satisfaction from seeing their victim suffer—this affirms their manhood.

- They justify their wrong acts in such a manner that makes them appear warranted and necessary.

- Their approach to life is "cutthroat." They believe "only the strong survive," and strength and control are synonymous to them.

- When they want or need something their philosophy is, "whatever it takes."

- They have super-sensitive egos. They will quickly challenge what they detect as an insult or mockery of their manhood.

- They disrespect others while insisting that others give them the utmost respect.

65

- They are driven by an insatiable desire to conquer and control. They see their desire for something as enough reason to acquire it any way that is necessary.

- They are self-absorbed and self-centered. Their primary concern is their satisfaction—all others take a back seat.

- They accept no responsibility for the sufferings of their victims. In fact, they blame their victims for their loathsome acts, saying "they were weak," "they are inferior," or "they shouldn't have been in the way."

- They are paranoid and skeptical of others. Their mistrustfulness of others paralyzes their ability to develop genuinely close relationships.

- They are haughty and high-minded. They feel others are beneath them. They see others as pawns to be used to satisfy their needs, wants and desires.

- They feel they are accountable to no one but themselves. They see themselves as the ultimate validator and legitimizer of their conduct.

WHITE RACISM IN THE BLACK MIND

How does the psychopathology of Black Gangsterism evolve? In *Black-on-Black Violence,* Dr. Amos Wilson discusses the "Internalization of White Racism by African Americans." Wilson writes:

> The introjection of eurocentrically falsified African images into the collective African American personality can only occur when African Americans themselves accept those falsified images as fact. Only when the lie is accepted as truth, only when a false projection is seen as a fact by virtue of its having been put forth by the ultimate validators of truth and reality, the ruling White Americans, can it be internalized and utilized by targeted African Americans to accordingly structure their personalities and interpersonal relations in ways that permit White American projected expectations to fulfill themselves.

Black gangsterism is the expression of White racist values internalized by Blacks. It is undoubtedly a degrading behavior. However, this behavior is the product of centuries of psychic, physical and cultural degradation. The "Black-on-Black" murderer represents one who expresses one of the two highest forms of Black self-degradation. Black suicide is the other.

66

The Black gangster's self-image is identical to the image his oppressor holds of him. As his oppressor, he does not see a man, rather a boy; he does not see an intelligent individual, rather a fool; he does not see a Black man or woman, he sees a nigga and a bitch; he does not see a Black human, rather he sees an animal such as a dog. The Black gangster embodies racism. In Psalms 17:21, the psalmist writes: As he *thinks* so is he. Because the Black gangster thinks like his oppressor, he treats himself and other Blacks as his oppressor. He essentially is the proxy for his oppressor. However, unlike his "psychological father," the Black gangster does not have political, economic or military power or the ability to draft policies and laws to exploit, rob and murder the "weak" and "inferior." Instead, he uses brute strength, knives and guns to victimize those he considers to be "weak" and "inferior"—Blacks.

GANGSTA RAP: WHITE RACISM WITH HIP-HOP FLAVA?

There is a gangsterism that is having injurious affects on African American psychology, young psychology in particular. This form of gangsterism is "gangsta rap." Gangsta rap is music that deals with sex, drugs, crime and violence in an extremely reckless manner. It is a psychosocial influence that seduces an individual's ego, imagination, desires and other psychological mechanisms and lures them into the dangerous social phenomenon called *gangsta*.

The "phenomenon of gangsta" is a powerful social/psychological dynamic that produces a regressive, materialistic, anti-intellectual and anti-aspirational culture. This culture creates a distinguishable bitterness of attitude, a unique slanguage—a language of slang—and style of dress, distinct hair styles, unique posturing and gestures, i.e., striking ways of walking, standing and staring. While young African American inner-city culture is deeply impacted by this phenomenon, its mark can be seen on White suburban and rural youth. Increasing numbers of White youth in these areas are modeling "gangsta behaviors." Suburban and rural White youth are forming gangs that are patterned after traditional urban Black gangs. Even many rural and suburban White youth who have little or no involvement with urban-styled gang members have that *gangsta* flare to their dress, gestures and speech.

Gangsta rap, which is also referred to as "genocide rap," and more recently "reality rap," is one of the many art forms in the repertoire of urban music known as "hip-hop." Hip-hop is more than a form of music. It is a high-spirited, music-centered culture that evolved in the mid-'70s through the turntable technology of three Black males named Afrika Bambaataa, Kool DJ Herc, and GrandMaster Flash in Harlem and Bronx, New York[15]. There are other categories of music under the hip-hop musical umbrella. They include political rap, party rap, new jack swing, Miami bass, etc.

Gangsta rap has been a lightning rod of controversy in America for nearly a decade. It is not the only controversial form of music in America, but it has been rebuked more than any other form of controversial music within the last decade. The Reverend Calvin Butts, C. Delores Tucker and the Reverend Jesse Jackson have spoken openly against this form of rap. There have even been Congressional hearings held concerning this music.

Many people enjoy rap music in general. It is the lethal flavor of gangsta rap lyrics that many people do not appreciate. However, it is understandable that gangsta rap has such strong appeal to young people. The rap artist's spicy style along with the poetic lyrics cast over a pulsating bass have riveting effects on the senses.

Gangsta rappers basically have six different thematic orientations. They include drugs, psychotic experiences, crime and violence, sexual promiscuity, materialism, and revolution. Revolution-oriented gangsta rappers, such as Ice Cube, possess enormous potential to steer young people's attention and energies toward liberation. Cube's ever evolving message of revolution is already compelling. It could be far more compelling if some specific modifications were made in the lyrics of some of his songs.

Many gangsta rap songs paint Blacks as gloriously criminal. Although many gangsta rappers say their intention is to "educate people about the ghetto," this music criminalizes the Black image. The promotion of this music is terribly dangerous in a day when members of the scientific establishment are weaving theories of linkages between violence and Black people's genes, and when government is rolling back the social and political gains of Blacks. This music helps set the atmosphere where the larger culture has little compassion for the regression of areas of Black progress. The gangsta rap industry is largely an anti-Black-progress, capitalist-motivated industry. Its songs glorify the legacies of African American oppression. A great deal of gangsta rap is White racism communicated in hip-hop slanguage through charismatic hip-hop personalities.

This brand of music promotes street culture which does not pose a real threat to White supremacy. All rap is not damaging, not even all rap songs made by gangsta rappers. The songs that are damaging however are those that handle the serious subjects of drugs, crime, violence and sexuality in a reckless and frivolous fashion. In *The Rap On Gangsta Rap*, Bakari Kitwana discusses the dynamic that sparked the evolution of gangsta rap out of hip-hop culture (rap). He writes:

> The influence of corporate elite commercialization on rap music must be considered in order to understand the various images of rap music. Rap music has been altered significantly and, more often than not, contaminated by this process of commercialization. This phenomenon is not specific to rap music, but is often the case when cultures and people are commodified. Rap music's increasing visibility

in addition to the increasing influence exerted onto rap by outside forces (i.e., corporate elite, academicians, politicians, and mass media) has found these original definitions redefined, most often in the best interest of the ruling elite.

Bakari Kitwana helps us understand that the capital-driven record industry elite saw tremendous financial opportunity in rap music. But Record companies were not concerned with preserving rap music as a meaningful, uplifting aspect of Black American culture. Neither were they concerned with rap being used as a vehicle of social and political liberation for Black people. Instead, their singular goal was to make money.

The result of pushing rap music out of the arms of Black culture onto the platform of popular culture was the creation of a distorted, regressive form of rap music which they labeled gangsta rap. The creation of this new genre of rap music generated a flood of young rappers competing vigorously for record deals from major record companies and an audience to perform for and sell records to. Shocking, degenerating language, and crude but captivating and sensational images became their primary means of achieving high sales.

THE LIE ABOUT MUSIC AND BEHAVIOR

As a student of musicology, I realize music is more than mere words or sounds, or the combination of words and sounds. Humans are creatures of rhythm and pulse. Music is based on these pulses in the human anatomy. Our bodies possess a natural rhythmic orientation. This causes our bodies to respond to pitches, beats, rhythms and cadences apart from our conscious participation. We impulsively snap our fingers, tap our toes, bounce our heads and feel certain emotions welling within us at the sound of certain kinds of music.

The notion that the impact of music goes no farther than the eardrum contradicts expert study and analysis of the physical, emotional and intellectual response to music. In *The Creation and Re-creation of Music,* David M. Keys states:

> The sense of music comes from the organization and presentation
> of sound waves. As a result our first response to music is often a
> physical one.

The belief that certain types of music or melodic combinations evoke physical and emotional responses is called the *doctrine of affections.* Practitioners of medicine are learning that music can be used as an effective instrument of healing. It stands to reason that music can likewise have detrimental affects on the human personality. In *The Rap On Gangsta Rap,*

Bakari Kitwana considers the issue of rap music's impact on Black youth perception and urban plight, and how they converge on their behavior. Kitwana writes:

> Given the extensive influence that rap artists maintain among black youth, perception of the use of guns are widely affected by these images. The tremendous amount of individual insecurity that persists among many black youth is articulated in some rap artists' justification of their need for weapons. The proliferation of guns in urban communities only serves to heighten such insecurities . . . While the existence of an underground economy in black urban America is not new, the availability of guns, the level of self-hatred, the quantity and potency of drugs, the unique insecurities, and the extreme black youth poverty all create a self-destructive situation unparalleled in black American history.

Scientific studies strongly suggest that music possesses hypnotic influences. Music creates an ambience and a climate that shape emotions, feelings and moods, which in turn encourage certain types of behavior. Our behavior confirms that we know this is true. When we want to engage in romance, we select music that fosters that mood, such as Luther Vandross. When we want to engage in spiritual activities, we select music that fosters that mood, such as Richard Smallwood or Maranatha Music. The opinion that music is merely words or sounds, or intermingled words and sounds that possess no power to influence moods and behavior, contradicts not just science, but our actions as well. Because music evokes certain emotions, parents who knowingly permit their children to listen to gangsta rap permit them to play a psychological version of the deadly game of Russian Roulette.

I think gangsta rap, like all forms of music, inspires behavior. In many instances violence is the inspired behavior. This inspiration does not occur simply because violence is a subject in these songs. The inspiration comes from the manner in which it is handled. There are two brands of violence, destructive and constructive. The brand of violence contained in most gangsta rap is the destructive brand. It is a violence that has no redeeming social value. Destructive violence leaves little babies dead in their homes from gunfire and places young Black males who have not reached the prime of their lives in prison for life.

Constructive violence entails all violence that has a meaningful purpose. This would include violence to protect oneself against physical attacks, or group violence in defense of an assault from another group. We would see dramatic changes in the African American community if all rappers condemned destructive violence and encouraged involvement in constructive violence only when it is necessary. Most gangsta rap songs and their videos, however, romanticize destructive violence and thereby indirectly sanction it.

Racist individuals use a number of justifications or rationalizations for their harmful behavior. The gangsta rapper does also. In the field of psychology, justifications and rationalizations are called *ego defense mechanisms*. An ego defense mechanism is a barrier that people erect in their minds and emotions in order to shield themselves from painful feelings, such as guilt, which arise because of some wrong they are involved in[16]. I believe most gangsta rappers know their music is damaging to their audience. Their words reflect the erection of ego defense mechanisms. Gangsta rappers can often be heard justifying their songs with remarks such as: "The violence was here before gangsta rap was around . . . know what I'm sayin'." And they rationalize their lyrics by saying: "Yo!, gangsta rap is just telling what's going on in the streets." Some of them are audacious enough to imply that it is all the parents' fault by saying: "Don't blame me for what parents don't do with [their] children." The commonly used remark: "I'm not a role model . . . it's not my responsibility to raise [your] children . . ." is indicative of how deeply the gangsta rapper is grounded in individualism.

The hip-hop culture has not been completely saturated with racist ideology. Many Black youth have been brought to social and political consciousness through the hip-hop culture. Hip-hop culture has spurred the creation of a political movement led by Black youth. Rappers such as Melle Mel, Chuck D/Public Enemy, KRS-One (Kris Parker), Queen Latifah, Arrested Development (Speech), De La Soul and X Clan have shown us that rap does not have to be profusely vulgar, genocidal, and misogynistic to sell. It can convey a strong message of Black upliftment and still be loved by the people. Gangsterism is a system of exploitation, thievery and perpetrating violence, psychic and/or physical, upon others for the express purpose of an individual or a group satisfying their needs or insatiable desires. Christopher Columbus, the European slave traders, White settlers of America, and the plantation owners represent those who placed profit above healthy human life. Gangsta rappers and their record labels do the same.

Six

Seduced by the Legal Institution: Chronicling Attacks on Black People by America's Legal System

In the summer of 1619, twenty Africans arrived in the "New World" aboard a European ship. They did not come directly from the African continent as "slaves," but from Europe as indentured servants. Indentured servants and slaves were not the same. Indentured servants provided labor in exchange for food and shelter while slaves were the property of the slave owner. During the mid-1660s, the colonies began legalizing the permanent enslavement of humans, particularly Africans. By 1776, more than 500,000 Africans were held in slavery and indentured servitude in the newly established United States of America[17].

A significant number of Africans lived in quasi-freedom; they were referred to as free Africans. The legalization of slavery affected the attitude Whites generally held toward free Africans. With slavery now a legal institution, they were now perceived by Whites as threats to society, more specifically threats to White economic growth. The national economy benefited tremendously from the exploitation of labor provided by enslaved Africans. Many Whites feared that free Africans would attempt to collapse the slave industry through subversion. They were also fearful that the free African's very existence would inspire enslaved Africans to engage in intense struggles for freedom. This fear generated a high degree of White animosity toward the community of free Africans in America.

WHITE FEARS OF AFRICAN FREEDOM TRIGGER ABUSES OF JUSTICE

After 1776, debates waged throughout the larger society over what would be the most effective solution to the free African dilemma. Two main solutions were placed on the table of debate. The first was the relocation of free Africans to unsettled American territory. The second was the deportation and colonization of free Africans on the African continent. United States Census Bureau figures reveal that in 1790 free Africans represented approximately 1.5 percent of the American population. Relocation would have been a time-consuming and costly endeavor.

By the early 1800s, deportation/colonization had become the most attractive solution to most ruling Whites to the free African dilemma. A Presbyterian clergyman from New Jersey, named Robert Finley, seized national enthusiasm regarding the deportation and colonization of free Africans. In 1817, Finley established an organization called the American Colonization Society (ACS). The birth of the ACS launched the Colonizationist Movement in America. Finley's ACS received major clergy and political support. It had an impressive list of members on its roster. They included Senator Henry Clay; Francis Scott Key, lawyer and composer of "The Star Spangled Banner"; Bushrod Washington, nephew of President George Washington; Supreme Court Clerk Elias B. Caldwell, and others. The ACS goal was two-fold. First, abolish international slave trading. Second, acquire land in Africa to colonize free Africans in America.

The ACS boasted of wanting to abolish the international trading of slaves. However, they were hypocritical in that they did not want to abolish the American institution of slavery. At its outset, the ACS made major strides toward accomplishing their goal. However, the organization was severely weakened by strong opposition from free African organizations and decreased support from affluent White merchants who were making huge profits off the gross exploitation of free African labor. By 1860, the ACS had deported 10,842 Africans to Liberia, Africa. However, support for the ACS began withering[18].

Although free Africans were an asset to some Whites, many Whites resented their presence. The dwindling support of "Plan A" (deportation/colonization), coupled with its slow drainage of free Africans out of America, prompted many Whites who were non-supportive of the ACS to draft "Plan B" to the free African problem. A plan was designed. The justice system would be used as an apparatus to regulate and control free African movement and progress in America. Local, state and federal legislators began drafting and passing laws that facilitated the easy arrest and incarceration of free Africans. The logic was simple: Since free Africans could not be colonized in Africa, colonizing them in America's jails and prisons could serve the same purpose.

The already corrupt enforcement of the law in the free African community worsened as time progressed. Jail and prison population statistics reflect the corrupt transformation of the justice system. During the 1820s, the representation of Blacks in the New York City jail and penitentiary systems fluctuated from one-quarter to two-thirds of the population. They only represented one-twelfth of the city's African population. During the 1830s and 1840s, free Africans in Baltimore, Maryland were approximately 17 percent of the population. However, the African jail percentile fluctuated from 25 to 34 percent.

The percentage of free Africans in America's prisons during much of the nineteenth century ranged from two to as much as six times higher than their population in the city. Free African status not only prescribed their arrest and incarceration, it also prescribed harsher and lengthier sentences than others. In 1849, a group of Quakers in Philadelphia observed that the sentences of free Africans:

> for crimes of the same grade are much longer, and very few in comparison with what whites have been discharged by pardon[19].

Free Africans were not the only Africans imprisoned. Enslaved Africans were incarcerated on the plantation in structures called slave pens. During the early years of slavery, plantation owners often used brutal beatings and lynchings to punish enslaved Africans. But they quickly realized that it was not good for their profit margin to damage their machinery beyond repair. They therefore constructed slave pens to incarcerate enslaved Africans. This punitive measure was often used in conjunction with severe, but non-fatal beatings.

The free African plight worsened as America drew closer to the Civil War, particularly in the South. White Southerners were obsessed with the fear that free Africans in the South would act as spies for the North to help them win the ensuing war. Consequently, the South passed laws to control free African movement that were more malicious. Even though crime was low in the free African community, jails and prisons still held disproportionately high numbers of free Africans. This disproportion was largely the result of Whites falsely accusing free Africans of crimes, legislators passing laws that facilitated their easy imprisonment, and a law enforcement system eager to arrest them. Observe the sampling of laws used to imprison free Africans:

- the inability to prove one's free status
- being unemployed
- not having a place to live
- witnessing a crime
- the inability to pay legal costs and fines accrued while in prison
- being accused of being a runaway
- violation of curfew
- looking out of a window

- exhibiting unsubmissive behavior
- speaking disrespectfully to a White person
- entertaining one another
- drinking alcohol
- congregating
- having unmarried sexual intercourse
- looking suggestively at a White woman
- attending religious services not authorized by the mayor
- walking in areas off limits to Blacks

THE HAUNTING GHOST OF CHATTEL SLAVERY

The exodus of more than four million Blacks from the clutches of American slavery into mainstream society posed a serious threat to the nation's status quo of White domination. Southern Whites were especially threatened by the influx of Blacks into the larger culture. They were humiliated and angered over their war defeat, because it robbed them of free labor that had provided them an ego boost and huge financial profits.

Emancipation and the Reconstruction brought a mixture of blessings and curses to Blacks in America. Although Blacks still were oppressed, they made major strides in politics, the justice system, civil rights legislation, etc. Those gains however, were quickly rolled back, and Whites, Southern Whites in particular, unleashed a powerful wave of race-motivated harassment and violence on Blacks. Thousands of Blacks were unlawfully jailed, imprisoned, emotionally terrorized, and murdered by the newly formed Ku Klux Klan and lynch mob gangs.

The American economy was largely dependent on agriculture at this period in history. The South was especially dependent upon it as its source of income. Therefore Southern Whites cunningly used the legal system to build a free labor system that would facilitate the exploitation of Black labor in the agricultural industry. Peonage and convict-leasing were created to ensure that the Southern agricultural industry remained under White control, and that it made large financial profits for White merchants.

Peonage involved Black sharecroppers agreeing to share their profits with White merchants in exchange for seed and equipment. Some Black sharecroppers were fortunate to profit under this agreement. However, most found themselves in debt to their lender. This debt accumulated not because Black sharecroppers were poor farmers—they were a hard-working people—but because White merchants maintained all financial records. Since many Black sharecroppers had poor reading skills, or none at all, White merchants falsified financial records to show Black sharecroppers in the red.

Southern lawmakers passed legislation making it illegal for Black sharecroppers to violate contractual agreements made with White lenders.

The consequence of this manipulative use of the law was that many Black sharecroppers found themselves being tried in court for breaking a financial agreement with a White lender. Conviction for the Black sharecropper was certain. Punishment entailed working for the White lender or being imprisoned.

Another system was designed to ensure White control over the agriculture-dependent Southern economy. It was known as "convict-leasing." This system involved prison officials leasing prison inmates to White merchants for a fee. Convict-leasing was a lucrative business practice. The money this enterprise paid politicians and prison officials through kickbacks from White merchants motivated officials to pressure law enforcers to make numerous arrests. Since the design of the legal system facilitated the easy arrest and imprisonment of Blacks, they became law enforcement's "bullseye target." Leased convicts worked for White merchants in workgangs. Workgangs were merely a legalized version of outlawed slavery. These systems increased the wealth of White merchants through the criminalization of Blacks, particularly the robust Black male.

The late 1800s introduced another legal apparatus by which Blacks could be controlled, criminalized and incarcerated. It was called Jim Crow. The Jim Crow concept actually originated in the North. However, White Southerners adopted it, enhanced it, and enforced it more passionately than their Northern counterparts. Jim Crow laws relegated Blacks to a lifestyle inferior to Whites. Their behavior and speech were regulated in every area of society including eating establishments, residential neighborhoods, public transportation, educational settings, health care facilities, places of lodging, and places of entertainment. Whites even felt Blacks were not fit to be buried in the same dirt as they. As a result of convict-leasing, peonage and Jim Crow, in 1899 the representation of Blacks in some Southern prison systems was as high as 90 percent[20].

THE MARK OF THE BEAST

By 1900, White perception of Blacks was severely defiled through decades of the press demonizing the Black image, and science trumpeting theories of Black crime being genetic. Whites thought the most vile and egregious crimes in America were being committed by urban Blacks. The press and scientific communities had indelibly marked the Black male as a brutal rapist. The press published highly exaggerated rape incidents involving Black men, most of which were not true. Scientists attributed the Black man's so-called uncontrollable craving to violate White women to their large phallic glands (penises). The press and scientists had done such a successful job of stamping Black males with the "mark of the beast," George Winston wrote:

When a knock is heard at the door, [the Southern woman] shudders with nameless horror. The black brute is lurking in the dark, a monstrous beast, crazed with lust. His ferocity is almost demonical. A mad bull or a tiger could scarcely be more brutal. A whole community is frenzied with horror, with the blind and furious rage for vengeance[21].

The mere accusation of raping a White woman guaranteed imprisonment for a Black man in the South, if he was not lynched first. Imprisonment and death could be the fate of Black men even when the rape accusations were known to be false. Between the 1890s and 1930s crime was low in the Black community. However, the image of Black men with large phallic glands lusting for White women incited inhumane acts of White violence.

Some 3,513 Blacks were known to have been lynched between the early 1880s and late 1920s[22]. The image of the savage brutal rapist caused Black male oppression to appear as though animals were being killed, not humans. The exact number of Blacks lynched will forever be a universal secret. In *A New Deal For Blacks*, Havard Sitkoff writes:

Petty brutality, lynchings and pogroms against the Negro section of towns occurred so frequently in the first decade of the twentieth century that they appeared commonplace, hardly newsworthy. Negro organizations recorded over a thousand lynchings of Southern blacks between 1900 and 1915. How many went uncounted no one can tell. No one today can even begin to estimate the number of blacks beaten, tortured, or killed by whites in those years. Nor can one describe adequately the terror of living with a constant fear of barbarity, of having your security subject to the whim of those who despise you, of having no recourse to police or courts.

BLACK RAGE TRANSFORMS INTO BLACK PROTEST

The Great Depression reopened the gates of race-motivated violence and injustice on Blacks. Attacking Blacks during economically distressful times was a common practice of Whites. Southern Blacks were especially worn out by the unrelenting attacks of Southern Whites. The savage murder of 14-year-old Emmett Till in latter August, 1955, was weighing heavily on the minds of Blacks. Till was shot through the head, severely bludgeoned about the body, and thrown into Mississippi's Tallahatchie River with a cotton gin fan wired about his neck. This incident helped crank the engine of the momentous movement of Black protest. However, the incident that put the vehicle of Black protest in drive occurred on December 1, 1955.

On this date a courageous Black woman decided to disobey the South's anti-Black Jim Crow law. Rosa Parks refused to relinquish her seat to a White man on a Montgomery, Alabama bus. The law demanded that every Black person abandon their seat to any White person who wanted it. Ms. Parks' arrest and jailing moved a group of local Black leaders in Montgomery to organize the Montgomery Bus Boycott. The brutal Till murder in Mississippi, and the Montgomery Bus Boycott, which lasted 381 days, launched the historic Black protest movement in America, a.k.a. The Civil Rights Movement.

An eloquent 26-year-old Baptist preacher named Martin Luther King, Jr. would become a notable figure in this historic movement. In response to this movement, the White supremacy system designed and executed the most insidious attacks by the justice system on Blacks, Black protest organizations and their leadership. King's civil activism and radical political position on the Vietnam war led to his untimely death on March, 1968, a victim of an assassin's bullet.

VICIOUS ATTEMPTS TO DESTROY BLACK PROTEST

In the early '60s, the Black protest movement caught the attention of FBI Director J. Edgar Hoover and other key governmental officials. It had reached a level of momentum that caused then to consider it a direct threat to the American status quo. Hoover decided to take a program that was in operation to crush the Communist structure in America and place it in the Black community. This program entailed intense surveillance, and the execution of a variety of extra-legal offensive tactics. Hoover wanted to paralyze Black protest in America. He considered any Black organization whose mission was to achieve civil and human rights for Blacks in "his America" a "black hate group."

Hoover and his Federal Bureau of Investigation often worked in cahoots with local law enforcement agencies harassing key Black leaders, maintaining surveillance on them, and arresting them and their followers for trumped-up charges and letter of the law violations.

A particularly well-known incident of malicious law enforcement on Black protesters was the June 1966 march to Jackson, Mississippi. James Meredith, the first African American to enroll in the University of Mississippi, started his "March Against Fear" on June 5, 1966 in Memphis, Tennessee. On the second day of his march, Meredith was injured by a sniper's bullet and was forced to discontinue his march. The Southern Christian Leadership Conference (SCLC) led by Dr. Martin Luther King Jr., the Student Non-violent Coordinating Committee (SNCC) led by Stokely Carmichael, and other Black organizations, committed to continuing the march for Meredith. Voter registration was added to the march, which traveled along Mississippi Highway 51. The registration of Black voters

SEDUCED BY THE LEGAL INSTITUTION

agitated the White power structure. As Whites were the minority in many Mississippi counties, the Black vote was a serious threat to their political power and control.

March leaders decided to rest for the night in a small town called Canton. They were granted permission by the Canton School Board to camp out for the night on school property. Tents were erected for shelter. White Canton officials hastened to prepare for their attack. First, White officials overrode the school board's decision permitting marchers to camp out on school property. Second, Mississippi State Troopers were dispatched to the campsite masked and armed with rifles and tear gas. King and Carmichael took a bold stance and decided not to abide by the city's racist-motivated repeal. State troopers pumped several containers of tear gas into the tents, causing marchers to gag, heave and pass out. Some marchers were injured by the flying metal containers. The troopers then rushed in and began kicking marchers and striking them with their rifle butts. Marchers were then arrested and placed in jail[23].

The program Hoover placed in the Black community was called the Counterintelligence Program or COINTELPRO. It was one of the supreme offensive weapons of the United States government used to undermine Black protest in America. For more than 14 years, COINTELPRO utilized a host of unlawful tactics against movement leaders and participants. These involved unlawfully monitoring the conversations of movement leaders, sending fraudulent letters to Black organizations to stir animosity, making illegal search warrants and unlawful arrests of Black activists, tampering with the cases of lawyers connected to the movement, creating the atmosphere for the murder of Black leaders, and a host of other strategies[24].

COINTELPRO tactics did not cease when the operation officially ended in 1971. In *How Capitalism Underdeveloped Black America*, political scientist and sociologist Manning Marable highlights:

> The Black Press Institute learned in November, 1981, that the Federal government was planning a series of grand jury hearings to explore "possible linkages between respected black organizations and terrorist groups." Using a little-used regulation to investigate the Mafia, the grand jury probe targeted civil rights organizations, Black social and cultural groups, community organizations and Black student groups.

JUSTICE IS STILL DENIED A PEOPLE

The struggle for Blacks in the era of "integration" is less for civil rights and more for economic empowerment and justice. The Joyce Ann Brown and William Bennett situations are demonstrations of justice denied. These two incidents are dramatic examples of justice obstructed by racism. But less severe incidents of injustice involving Blacks occur every day in America.. Black media report many of these stories, but most go uncovered.

The reason for the frequency of such incidents is that the original purpose of the policing system was not to protect and serve the African American community, but to control them by any means necessary. In many ways the control of the African American community is still the supreme function of the police in the African American community—not protection and service.

JOYCE ANN BROWN
DALLAS, TEXAS

Ruby Kelley was reading the Dallas Morning News on May 9, 1980 when she saw a picture of her daughter, Joyce Ann Brown. Ms. Kelley read the article that accompanied her daughter's picture and discovered that she was a suspect in a robbery and murder incident at a Dallas furrier. The event had occurred on May 6th at approximately 1 p.m. She quickly called her daughter to tell her that the police wanted her for robbery and murder. Brown thought it was a joke at first. However, she became dismayed after realizing her mother was serious. Once the shock subsided, she decided to go the police station to rectify this problem. Brown was certain the situation would be quickly resolved and she would leave the station a cleared woman.

Brown went to the station and was arrested immediately upon identifying herself. Dallas police began investigating their case. They discovered that the car used in the offense was rented by a woman named Joyce Ann Brown. However, this Joyce Ann Brown rented the car from a rental company in Denver, Colorado. The police spoke with this Joyce Ann Brown who told them that she let a woman named Renee Taylor use the car. Credible witnesses told police that the Dallas Joyce Ann Brown was at work at the time of the offense. (By a strange coincidence Brown worked at a furrier business.) However, the police proceeded with their investigation despite the strong evidence that suggested Brown was not their suspect.

In the course of their investigation the police also discovered that Renee Taylor had robbed furrier businesses in other states. They executed a search warrant on her apartment and found furs, a .22 caliber revolver that had been discharged, and a jogging suit that matched the one the perpetrator purportedly wore. Taylor's fingerprints were also found on the getaway vehicle. Police searched Brown's Dallas home and found no evidence that could tie her to the offense. Despite the compelling evidence pointing to Brown's innocence, Dallas police charged her with the crime.

Brown's criminal trial began Tuesday, September 30, 1980. She felt hopeful that the trial would reveal that this was a strange case of mistaken identity. Things looked favorable for Brown until the murder victim's widow took the stand. In a tearful testimony she identified Brown as the robber who wore the pink jogging suit.

The defense scored high points when they demonstrated that it was impossible for Brown, who on the day of the offense wore a white skirt and black blouse, to change clothes, drive to the furrier in afternoon rush hour traffic, commit the offense, drive back to work in afternoon rush hour traffic, change clothes and start working without being late. The prosecution countered the defense's strategy with the testimony of a surprise witness. Martha Jean Bruce, Brown's cell mate, testified that Brown boasted about committing the offense. Bruce had two prior convictions for lying to police, but this was not brought up in the trial. On October 23, 1980 the all-White Dallas jury rendered a guilty verdict of aggravated robbery. Joyce Ann Brown was sentenced to life in prison.

Private investigators were able to gather solid and convincing information proving that Martha Jean Bruce perjured herself on the stand. After serving nine years in Mountain View Prison, Brown was set free. One month following Brown's trial, Martha Jean Bruce received a reduction in her sentence for criminal attempt murder[25].

WILLIAM BENNETT
BOSTON, MASSACHUSETTS

On October 23, 1989, Charles Stuart, a 29-year-old White attorney, made a frantic emergency call to Boston police. He reported that he and his seven-month pregnant wife, Carol Stuart, had been shot near the Mission Hill neighborhood of Boston. While on the phone with police, Stuart told the dispatcher that his wife died. When police arrived, Carol Stuart was dead from a gunshot wound to the head, and Charles Stuart had a gunshot wound to his stomach.

Stuart reported that a Black man jumped into their car as he and his wife were leaving child birth class at Brigham Women's Hospital. He said the perpetrator then forced him to drive to a deserted area near Mission Hill and robbed them of jewelry, some keys, and his wife's purse. Stuart then told police that the robber panicked after mistaking his cell phone for a police radio. He then shot him and Mrs. Stuart, and left running. Emergency units rushed Carol Stuart to the hospital so the baby could be delivered by c-section. Unfortunately, it died two weeks later. The baby's death moved the DA's office to upgrade the charges to a double homicide.

This violent Black-on-White crime sent the press into a frenzy. The state's legislature began demanding the reinstatement of the death penalty. The mayor ordered 100 extra police to saturate the predominantly Black Mission Hill, Dorchester and Roxbury neighborhoods. The police culminated their search for the brutal murderer with the arrest of 39-year-old William Bennett. It was reported that Charles Stuart identified Bennett in a line-up. Witnesses stated in their affidavit that Bennett told them he committed the crime. The police were proud that they had captured this dangerous criminal. However, their pride soon withered into shame. On January 3, 1990, Charles Stuart's brother, Matthew, contacted Boston police and told them that Charles Stuart was the killer.

Carol Stuart's wedding ring was handed over to police by a relative of Stuart. This was the ring Stuart said the Black perpetrator stole. This piece of jewelry gave the police grounds to arrest Stuart. Before Stuart could be arrested, he killed himself by jumping off the Tobin Bridge. The police later found Mrs. Stuart's purse, and the revolver used to kill her, in a river near their home. It was also reported that the police coerced witnesses into giving false statements on their affidavits. William Bennett is living proof that Black criminalization is still a reality in the 1990s[26].

When interviewed for this book, Joyce Ann Brown told me: "At least six percent of people convicted of crimes in America are innocent." Some may say six percent is not a lot of people. But we must realize that this is 6 percent of people [convicted] of crimes, not detained or arrested by police, placed in jail, or tried in a court of law.

Many Americans hold the justice system in high regard. They find it hard to believe that the system is saturated with flaws and failures. A 1993 Congressional study entitled *Innocence and the Death Penalty* made a chilling revelation. It reported that: "A substantial number of death row inmates are indeed innocent." If there are "substantial" failures on the most critical level of the criminal justice process, how many failures are there on levels below capital trial? The study went on to say that: "There is a high risk that some of them will be executed."

One might be tempted to say that if Joyce Ann Brown had been wealthy or well-known, her fate would certainly have been different. This thought is not valid at all. High-profile Blacks make prime targets for public humiliation and the facilitation of Black disorganization through criminalization. Marcus Garvey, W.E.B. Dubois, Martin Luther King Jr., Paul Robeson, Sonny Liston, Muhammad Ali, Louis Farrakhan, Quabila Shabazz, Michael Jackson, Mike Tyson and O.J. Simpson did not escape it. The political or activist spotlight does not guarantee protection either. Marion Barry, Alcee Hastings and other prominent Black political figures are examples of that.

SEVEN

JUSTICE OR JUSTIFIED OPPRESSION?

The state prison population increased 58 percent in
5 years but remained mostly male, minority, and young.

Bureau of Justice Statistics
Survey of State Prison Inmates, 1991

The breakthroughs African Americans have made in politics and the criminal justice system over the past 25 years have been impressive. This is especially notable considering the varied attempts Whites made to thwart these efforts. The section of the criminal justice system where African Americans have experienced significant progress is law enforcement. African Americans comprise 53.3 percent of Detroit's police department. In Atlanta, the city of the first African American female chief, and Washington, D.C., Blacks comprise 54.6 percent and 67.8 percent of their police departments respectively. With regard to politics, African Americans occupy more than 7,900 elected positions[27].

The question we must ask ourselves is: Now that African Americans occupy high and low positions within America's political and justice systems, are they receiving justice? Many Whites would respond with a resounding YES! They draw this conclusion based on legislative victories attained through Black litigation and protestation of the '50s and '60s; the opening of locked doors in mainstream society that permitted some African Americans to rise to middle-class status. However, on the other side of this coin is the experience of a measurable segment of the African American community. This group are being "justifiably oppressed" by the criminal justice machine. For purposes of this book, justified oppression means:

85

the criminal justice system's usage of Black crime and mythology to rationalize and justify its discriminative and abusive treatment of law-abiding and law-offending Blacks.

RODNEY KING: A ROYAL EXAMPLE

One of the most poignant examples of justified oppression was the March 3, 1991 beating of Rodney King by Los Angeles police officers. This incident—more typical than most people realize—was captured on videotape by an onlooker named George Holliday. King was struck 56 times with P152 batons and shot with two 50,000-volt Taser darts as several officers stood nearby gawking. The officers justified their actions claiming that striking King incessantly for one minute and 21 seconds, and shooting him with two 50,000-volt Taser darts was necessary to contain him—even though other officers stood nearby. King suffered numerous fractures to the face, a broken leg and serious emotional damage[28].

In the trial of California v. Powell, former LAPD Sergeant Stacy Koon testified that his treatment of King was determined by the fact that he was a man of large stature. He said this indicated to him that King may have been an ex-convict (inmates often lift weights while incarcerated). Koon also testified that King's odd behavior led him to believe that he was dealing with a man on the potent drug called PCP.

The Los Angeles police department's P152 baton instructor testified as an expert witness and gave his "blow-by-blow" take on the beating. He explained to the jury that because King did not stop moving his legs and arms after repeated commands, the four officers' safety was threatened. (Wouldn't the P152 instructor move his legs if he were being beaten by those hard sticks?) He testified that he believed the officers were in compliance with Los Angeles police department use of force policy when they struck King 56 times with their batons.

The defense capitalized on three factors of the beating episode as justifications for the officer's conduct. First, King fled from the officers in his Hyundai when they initially tried to stop him. Second, King resisted the officers when he was approached by them. Third, King was a convicted felon[29]. In the final analysis, these factors helped the mostly-White Simi Valley jury return from deliberations with a not guilty verdict, thus justifying oppression.

THE CONCEPT OF INSTITUTIONAL CRIMINALIZATION

Civil rights and equal opportunity under the law for Blacks in America were the principal objectives of the historic civil rights movement. Although these issues are still important, two more issues demand the concern of the collective Black American community. These issues are economic power and justice. Segments of the African American community are being criminalized by the institution of criminal justice in addition to being justifiably oppressed.

Institutional criminalization and justified oppression are similar concepts, but they have distinct differences. The concept of institutional criminalization is: a systematic process in which the institution of criminal justice strictly enforces the law on, and employs severe measures to illegitimately and legitimately arrest Blacks and process them through the justice system labeling them criminal.

Justified oppression and institutional criminalization are distinguishable by their outcome. Racial/economic-motivated discrimination and physical abuse by members of the justice system are the trademarks of justified oppression, while racial/economic-motivated arrest, legal and unlegal, by members of the justice system is the trademark of institutional criminalization.

It is difficult for many people to see these processes in operation. The actual seriousness of Black crime places a huge blindfold over their "mental eye." In fact, the seriousness of Black crime coupled with misleading crime/ arrest reports, discussion of Black violence being genetic by so-called notable figures, and the visual impact of exotic violent Black images cause many people to think the justice system is too weak and too soft on Black crime. This reality provides politicians a platform to stomp on in their solicitation for votes. In fact politicians who do not speak the tough on crime language commit political suicide.

This belief also allows the criminal justice system to assume a more aggressive posture in Black communities without coming under serious public scrutiny. Police departments design "tough" and "innovative" strategies to crack down on urban crime. The courts decide to send "criminals" a message and give Blacks stiffer sentences. One thing is forgotten in all this. Crime is serious in America, not just Black America.

BLACK PEOPLE SUBSCRIBE TO THEIR OPPRESSION

Another variable that justifies the criminal justice system's abuse and discriminative delivery of justice to African Americans is the demands of African Americans. African Americans nationwide are demanding more intense responses from the criminal justice system to crime in their community. ABC's *Nightline* aired a program on February 15, 1995 that dealt with a bill drafted by United States Representative Bill McCollum, chairman of the Crime Subcommittee. This bill would essentially relax the exclusionary rule in order to give law enforcement authorities more room to make warrantless searches under certain circumstances. On this same program, ABC shared the results of a study conducted to determine how willing Americans were to relinquish some of their rights in exchange for safety. The poll revealed the level of panic Americans felt about crime and violence. It showed that 51 percent of Americans would "trade some freedoms for safer streets." I think it would be safe to assume that many, if not most, of the individuals polled were White. If this assumption is true, the poll sends a chilling message to Blacks. If Whites would be willing to trade some of their freedoms for safer streets, how do you think they feel about the freedoms of Blacks?

Black demands on the justice system to get tough on crime are made with good intentions. However, when the system gets "tough on crime," many Black communities fail to do two things. First, they fail to closely monitor the system's treatment of Blacks. Second, they fail to demand that the system deliver stern and fair justice ever. Studies verify that the effect of these so-called "tough on crime initiatives" often result in African Americans representing the highest percentage of people being processed through the justice system.

The abuse and discriminative delivery of justice to African Americans is worsening. These conditions are not blatantly obvious to many Americans because their vision is blurred by two things: first, the exaggerated seriousness of crime and violence in the African American community as depicted by mass media; second, reality television shows such as *Rescue 911*, *The Highway Patrol*, *The Judge*, *Cops*, etc. These shows project a boy scout image of American justice. Hence, when governmental and law enforcement agencies draft crime initiatives involving the police executing high volumes of narcotic search warrants on dime and quarter crack houses and zero tolerance strategies that target Blacks; and when police abuse Blacks, it is perceived as the state responding to the demands of Blacks. What better way to mistreat a people than to do so with their demand.

DOUBLE STANDARDS IN CRIMINAL JUSTICE

White Americans, particularly the conservative right, say much about the unfairness of "selective" and "double standard" social policies and programs that benefit Blacks and not Whites. However, they say little about double standards in the delivery of justice that benefit them and not Blacks. Whites commit far greater numbers of crime in America than Blacks; yet Blacks find themselves occupying more jail and prison beds in America. Moreover, there are fewer executions of zero tolerance strategies, street sweeps and drug search warrants in White communities than in Black neighborhoods on balance. Below is a list of 13 consequences of double standards in the delivery of justice:

- less regard for the rights of Blacks guaranteed by the Constitution
- disproportionate rates of Black arrests

- overcharging Black offenders
- disparity in Black incarceration populations
- bond practices that are unfair to Blacks
- Blacks being denied work release more often than Whites
- higher rates of conviction for Blacks than others
- fewer deferred adjudications for Blacks
- fewer plea bargain offers made for Blacks
- fewer probations granted for Blacks
- lengthier prison sentences given to Blacks
- higher rates of incarceration for Blacks
- fewer paroles for Blacks

Because crime and violence are serious problems in many Black communities, increasing numbers of Blacks are reshaping their attitudes and relations with police. It was only two decades ago that police were menaces in African American communities. This change in relationship may not be a bad move in every city. Many police departments are making the needed transition from merely policing the African American community to serving them as well. Police "service" had always been the lost dimension in police work in the African American community.

Although there is still much room for improvement in police service, the improvements some departments have made are the result of community policing concepts that enhance the service component of police work. The product of enhanced police service is improved Black community and police relations, which often leads to more effective law enforcement.

An atmosphere of cooperation is created when the police balance enforcement with service. When police decide they are going to "clean up the hood" without establishing good relations with the people, the citizenry suffers. In these situations, Blacks generally resist ultra-aggressive enforcement tactics by police. Consequently, many officers become antagonistic and respond more aggressively to Black criminals. Innocent Blacks are often violated and criminalized in this process.

Poor Black community/police relations has been a problem largely because of the type of officers that are assigned to work in Black neighborhoods. The typical officer graduating from the police academy is a White male who has been raised in the suburbs, or in a predominantly White neighborhood, who possesses little or no experience in relating with Blacks. To many of these officers working in the African American community is more of a sport than a service. The opening of doors for African Americans to enter the field of law enforcement has brought an Africentric perspective to policing that is vital to effective and productive police service in the African American community.

FALSE PERCEPTIONS GENERATE TWO BRANDS OF JUSTICE

The seriousness of crime in the African American community is often used by Whites to counter Black allegations of discrimination in the administration of justice. The mass media support this counter-argument with shocking images of Blacks who appear to be addicted to crime and violence. Centuries of portraying Blacks as super-criminals has made it difficult for people to look at Blacks without their mental eye being covered with the tint of crime.

Because America perceives Blacks as criminals, particularly urban Blacks, when Americans put on blue uniforms, blue pinstriped suits and black robes to deliver justice, the product is a brand of American justice called "Black justice." Black justice is less tolerant and more punitive than White justice. It is justice that has been contaminated with racial bias, false perceptions, socioeconomic bias, racism and politics.

Double standard justice can be seen in crack and cocaine laws. The penalty for the possession of 500 grams of powder cocaine, which is valued at approximately $40,000, is the same for the possession of 5 grams of crack cocaine, which is valued at approximately $250. Powder cocaine is a popular drug in White communities, while crack cocaine is a popular drug in inner-city Black communities.

The effects of double standards in the delivery of justice are more clearly demonstrated in a study conducted by the State of Texas Criminal Justice Policy Council (February 1994). It examined arrest and sentencing dynamics in the state of Texas by race. Here are some of the findings:

ARRESTS IN TEXAS: 1985 AND 1992

- The number of African American arrestees rose from 51,888 in 1985 to 70,617 in 1992—a 36 percent increase.

- African American arrests increased from 1985 to 1992, particularly among drug arrestees. The number of African American drug arrestees increased 95 percent from 12,159 to 23,653.

VIOLENT CRIMES

- African American offenders comprised the largest proportion of offenders convicted in each category (homicide, sexual assault, robbery and assault) *except* sexual assault, and comprised the majority of offenders convicted for robbery.

DRUGS

- The majority of offenders convicted for a drug felony were African American at 57 percent—followed by:

  Anglo - 27 percent
  Hispanic - 16 percent

SENTENCING

- Overall, 49 percent of all felons received a sentence to prison:

  57 percent of African American felons
  45 percent of Hispanic felons
  40 percent of Anglo felons

- 26 percent of all felons received deferred adjudication:

  32 percent of Anglo felons
  25 percent of Hispanic felons
  21 percent of African American felons

- Over 50 percent of African American drug offenders in each category (possession, delivery, and manufacturing) received a prison sentence.

- A larger proportion of African American offenders received a prison sentence than Anglo offenders convicted for cocaine possession.

- A larger percentage of African American offenders were sentenced to prison in each offense category (homicide, sexual assault, robbery, and assault) than Anglos or Hispanics.

IMPRISONMENT

- The percentage of African Americans in the Texas prison system in 1992 was four times their percentage representation in the state adult population.

- In 1985, the convicted felon to prison rate for African Americans was 5.5 times higher than the convicted felon to prison rate for Anglos. By 1992 the convicted felon to prison rate for African Americans was nine times higher than that of Anglos.

Numerous studies have been conducted to determine whether racial bias and racism are dynamics that influence the criminal justice process. In her book *Don't Believe The Hype*, Farai Chideya writes:

> According to the Federal Judicial Center, in 1990 the average sentences for blacks on weapons and drug charges were 49 percent longer than those for whites who had committed and been convicted of the same crimes—and that disparity has been rising over time.

An article in the 1993 *USA Monitor* written by Al Brown provides more evidence of racism influencing criminal justice. Brown's article discusses the findings of a Minnesota task force formed to determine whether race was a factor affecting the delivery of Minnesota's criminal justice process. The 36-member task force compiled data for analysis through surveys, public hearings, major studies and focus group interviews. The study group was called the Supreme Court Racial Bias Task Force. Their report substantiated that racial bias does influence Minnesota's criminal justice system. Here are some of the task force findings:

- People of color are disproportionately caught up in the criminal justice system. The state's non-white population is six percent, but yet the non-white prison population is 45 percent.

- People of color make up only 11 percent of Hennepin County's population however, they account for 53 percent of the most serious felonies.

- People of color were more than twice as likely to be arrested for the most serious crimes. But once charged they were twice as likely to have the charges dismissed outright, indicating there may have been insufficient grounds for picking them up in the first place.

- In Hennepin County, whites are more likely to receive a summons and African Americans are more likely to be arrested for the same offense.

- Some criminal justice system professionals believe there is a pattern of racial disparity in plea bargaining. Thirty percent of metro judges younger than 50 say that with all factors being equal, white defendants are more likely to see favorable plea bargains.

- Minnesota's incarceration rate for African Americans is 16 times higher than that for whites.

- In Hennepin County, whites are more likely to receive a fine and people of color are more likely to receive a jail sentence for misdemeanor crimes of assault, prostitution and theft, even though they are convicted of the same offense and have similar criminal histories.

According to a report by the United States Sentencing Commission, non-Whites were prosecuted for crack-related offenses in more than half of federal courts despite the fact that Whites use and sell crack cocaine in greater numbers than non-Whites. In fact, 17 states have not prosecuted a single White in federal court. The commission also reported that Whites who sell crack are generally prosecuted in state court. The consequence of being prosecuted in federal court versus state court is a lengthier sentence. Federal District Court Judge Consuelo B. Marshall stated: "We do see a lot of these cases and one does ask why some are in state court and some are being prosecuted in federal court. And if it's not based on race, what's it based on?"

THE INFLUENCE SOCIOECONOMICS HAS ON THE JUDICIAL PROCESS

The treatment one receives from the judicial system is influenced not only by race, but by socioeconomic status. Only 18 percent of white-collar embezzlers go to prison, and the average time spent is 15 months. In fact, many of their sentences are dropped. On the flip side, 89 percent of working poor people convicted of larceny spend an average of 10.5 years behind bars. The information below shows that Blacks serve more time in jail than Whites for the same offenses[30].

CRIME	BLACKS	WHITES
Murder	91.7 months	79.8 months
Rape	55.0 months	43.9 months
Kidnaping	41.0 months	37.0 months
Robbery	37.4 months	33.3 months

New York Supreme Court Judge Bruce Wright gives profound insight into the American legal system with his book entitled *Black Robes, White Justice*. The judge cites a situation involving an upper-income White and lower-income Black defendant. This incident is a golden example of racial/socioeconomic bias influencing the judicial process. Judge Wright writes:

Earlier in his career on the federal bench, Cooper (Federal Judge Irving Ben Cooper of New York) had been called upon to sentence two defendants, one white, one black. The white defendant was a former Wall Street broker. He had been convicted of illegally selling stocks. He had collected a commission of some $250,000, which he laundered through a secret Swiss bank account. He had perjured himself before the federal grand jury that investigated him.

Judge Cooper remarked that the well-dressed defendant was not likely to repeat such an act. He fined him $90,000 and placed him on probation for a year. Simple subtraction may reveal that, in that case at least, crime did pay. When Judge Cooper sentenced the black man, however, prison was on his mind. The black man, the sole supporter of a diabetic wife and daughter, was a truck driver. He had been convicted of stealing a television set from the truck he drove. It was a black-and-white set worth less than $100. The judge sent him to jail for a year.

THE AMERICAN PRISON SYSTEM:
A PARTNER IN THE PERPETUATION OF CRIME

Prisons overall do not rehabilitate offenders. Instead, the prison experience induces many offenders deeper into criminality. Statistical data from the state with one of the highest rates of incarceration in America affirms this. There are 118,000 people behind bars in the Texas prison system. This equates to one out of every 156 Texas residents. Half of them had been previously incarcerated. The number of penitentiaries in the United States has doubled since 1980 to more than 1,300, but 30 states are still experiencing overcrowding. It costs six times more in 1995 than it did in 1975 to operate state and federal penitentiaries. Today Americans will spend $24 billion to finance them[31].

A report by the Texas Department of Criminal Justice Institutional Division on prison violence speaks to the ineffectiveness of penitentiaries. It reports that there were 1,555 inmate assaults, 5,598 staff assaults and 52 inmate homicides in 1984 and 1985. There were more inmate homicides in those two years than in the previous 15 years combined. The recidivism rate also underscores the ineffectiveness of our current prison system. A Bureau of Justice Statistics study entitled *Recidivism of Young Parolees* reports:

> Recidivism rates were highest in the first two years after an offender's release form prison. Within one year, 32 percent of those paroled had been rearrested; within two years, 47 percent had been rearrested.

Genuine rehabilitation does not occur in prison because society uses incarceration for the wrong reasons. It is used primarily to isolate and manipulate offenders, and deter crime. Correcting attitudes and behavior is not a major goal. The perception of offenders as predators inhibits the creation of meaningful programs that deal with matters of the heart and soul of offenders. No value is placed on bringing inmates to an awareness of themselves through counseling, education and spirituality.

This problem is compounded by a society that offers few opportunities for ex-convicts. People lobby for the delivery of harsher punishments and larger prisons, but say little or nothing about the existence of social variables that help generate criminality. Consequently, inmates outnumber prison beds, a condition that leads to the spillage of non-rehabilitated offenders into free society. Society is now paying for its attitude that "the only thing society owes a criminal is a prison bed or voltage" with victimization by prison parolees who have not been rehabilitated.

The word penitentiary derives from the term penitent, which means to be repentant. Prison culture does not evoke repentance. It is a minute-by-minute struggle with a host of bitter experiences that evoke bitter emotions. Prison culture cheapens human life. This is felt even more by Black prisoners who are trapped in walls of bitter racism. Inmates endure daily exercises of dehumanizing rituals. The foul blend of human waste and body odor become rude wake-up calls. Intrusive body-cavity searches insult and humiliate. The echoing wails of rape victims are loud declarations of their utter vulnerability. Prison culture suffocates the spirit. It demoralizes inmates because society labels certain criminals as predators. Prisons are therefore more oriented in treating inmates as animals and beasts, not as individuals in need of rehabilitation.

The CBS program *60 Minutes* aired a program on September 12, 1993 that dealt with the Pelican Bay State Prison in California. This prison facility has a special section within its unit called the Security Housing Unit or the SHU. This unit is set apart strictly for violent inmates. The operation and physical design of the SHU hammers the mind. Inmates do not have access to direct sunlight or contact with other inmates. They are kept under 24-hour surveillance by armed guards and are permitted to leave their cells only 1.5 hours a day to shower and exercise. There have been numerous complaints by SHU inmates of unnecessary uses of force by prison guards.

The Pelican Bay SHU is nothing more than a high-tech torture chamber. This institution has driven inmates into dementia. Our failure to address prison systems of this nature is suicidal. After inmates are violated by these systems, they are released from prison to violate others.

Should our society have Pelican Bay SHU facilities? Are these kinds of facilities capable of rehabilitating offenders? Is the Pelican Bay SHU an example of the fair delivery of justice, or is it merely another example of justified oppression? America must realize that when there is no justice, there will be no peace.

THE AMERICAN PRISON SYSTEM:
THE BILLION-DOLLAR INDUSTRIAL COMPLEX

In the latter '80s African Americans were alarmed to hear that one in four African American males in their 20s were supervised by the criminal justice system. A little more than five years later, the United States Sentencing Project reports that one in three African American males in their 20s are supervised by the criminal justice system. The numbers continue to get bleaker. One in 14 African American males is incarcerated, and African American males are eight times more likely to be incarcerated than White males.

What are we to think of these numbers? Has crime within African American male culture risen in the '90s? Are African American males committing eight times more crimes than White males? The seriousness of crime in young African American male culture is irrefutable. However, these numbers are being driven to astonishing heights by racism and economics, in addition to increases in African American male criminality.

In chapter one, *Lies and Half Truths about Crime in the Black Community*, it was explained that the influence of racism and discrimination within the justice system render crime statistics an unreliable tool of accurate crime measurement in America. The same rule applies to prison statistics. They, too, reflect the influence of racism and discrimination in the criminal justice system, as well as the economic incentive to have an expanding prison complex.

According to the Justice Department, America currently has more than 1.1 million bodies in prison. A disproportionate number of them are African American. African Americans are being seduced into crime and violence, then disproportionately arrested and incarcerated. Once in prison, African American labor is exploited by booming prison corporations. (This is reminiscent of the old money making convict-leasing system of the late 1800s.)

The privately operated prison industrial complex is currently a $250 million-a-year industry. Nearly 20 states have privately operated prisons; federal prisons will be going private also. The state of Texas currently has the highest number of privately operated prison facilities in the nation, totaling more than 30. With prisoners being paid less than $1 dollar an hour for labor that generates billions of dollars in profit, there is greater incentive to lean more heavily toward enforcement and incarceration than toward prevention.

Many federal prisons have factories operated by prisoners. Prisoners manufacture a number of items, including license plates, highway signs, furniture, and boxes. Some even do telemarketing and reservations for large corporations.

The replacement of manual labor with automation, the demand for laborers skilled in high technology, and the loss of jobs exported to foreign countries has many cities economically distressed. However, tremendous hope has been placed in the emergence of the billion-dollar prison industry. A single prison facility can provide a city with hundreds of jobs with attractive pay and benefits. A prison guard can earn more than $40,000 a year. There is also money to be made outside the prison facility. Contractors stand to make billions in prison construction.

What are the consequences of a billion-dollar prison industrial complex in the African American community? Crime control and incarceration will be considered the most effective solution to crime. Monies for crime prevention will dry up. A marked increase in the percentage of African Americans in prisons can then be anticipated.

Economic incentive will motivate private prisons to prolong the stay of some prisoners. Already inept rehabilitation programs can be expected to plunge to lower levels of ineptitude. An unfeeling prison environment that further hardens prisoners will develop because the inmate will be seen as a commodity. Inmates will likely become involved in crime upon release due to increased hardening and a society that offers them decreasing economic opportunities.

A people cannot survive when increasing numbers of their men are being socially, politically and economically castrated. This is especially true in a capitalistic society such as America. The scene in the movie *Waiting To Exhale* where Savannah, Bernadine, Robin and Gloria are sitting on the floor citing the laundry list of reasons they could not find a "good Black man" as they sipped on a glass of wine will become distressingly more common if African American males continue coming under the control of the criminal justice system.

HOW DO OFFICERS SUCH AS FORMER LOS ANGELES POLICE DEPARTMENT DETECTIVE MARK FUHRMAN STAY ON THE POLICE DEPARTMENT?

The trial of the People v. Simpson was the "Pandora's box" of the American system of justice. This trial scraped the glossy facade off the institution of criminal justice and exposed its corruption. Two of the multiple issues the Simpson trial pressed to the face of America were racist law enforcement officers (Mark Fuhrman), and police misconduct. These issues ranked highest on the scale of national attention and concern.

The issue of police misconduct and corruption is old hat to African Americans. This was demonstrated in chapter three, *Oppressive Strategies that Seduce Blacks into Crime*. The Fuhrman tapes were a deja vu experience for many African Americans, particularly males. The visceral shock these tapes evoked was felt primarily by Whites. The shock and surprise Whites expressed over them manifests two realities. First, Whites largely deny a more than minor existence of racism in America's law enforcement system. Second, Whites discount the protestations and grievances of Blacks regarding their victimization by police.

Police misconduct and corruption are subjects worthy of a much larger study. This essay will examine a few of the multitudinous variables that contribute to them. No one can say exactly how many corrupt officers there are on America's police departments. A singular act of police misconduct is not necessarily the sign of a corrupt officer. Some police misconduct occurs because officers give in to the base elements of their human nature for a brief moment. For purposes of this essay, a "corrupt officer" is defined as an officer who intentionally and willfully uses his or her power and authority to injure or violate others with some degree of consistency.

Inasmuch as people want police to be perfect, we must realize that police, like other people, are challenged by personal and professional difficulties. Officers therefore can exhibit rudeness or anger as other people do under stressful situations. The intense pressure of police work sometimes pushes individuals beyond their boundaries. It peels the facade off their personality, exposing their weaknesses. When these weaknesses are exhibited while on active duty, the behavior is called police misconduct. The factor of human weakness is not offered to justify police misconduct but merely to consider as a variable that produces police misconduct.

The existence of police misconduct and corruption are grave issues. However, the failure of the police system to purge departments of officers known to be corrupt is an issue of greater gravity. Police misconduct is multicausal. Some of the causes include: 1) the standard recruit personality profile, 2) academy training and socialization, 3) overwhelmed by power, 4) police culture, 5) harsh street experiences, 6) racism, 7) fear and anxiety, and 8) politics.

1. THE STANDARD RECRUIT PERSONALITY PROFILE

Police departments generally seek to recruit individuals with aggressive personalities. Psychological screening to weed out applicants with serious psychological and emotional problems has been a facet of the hiring process since the mid-'60s. However, the results often are not fully reliable. Many recruits who appear to merely have aggressive personalities are among those high in citizen complaints filed against them and/or are the regular subjects of Internal Affairs investigations of serious acts of misconduct.

2. ACADEMY TRAINING AND SOCIALIZATION

Once a recruit becomes a candidate, he is socialized through the training process to be more aggressive. In a paper entitled *Psychological Screening as it Relates to Police Misconduct* (1991), Fort Worth police department Sergeant Janice Willingham explains this phenomenon. She writes:

> Police training involves defensive tactics, such as hand to hand combat, use of the police koga baton and shooting techniques. Subsequently, because of the training, a transformation of beliefs

and attitudes of the candidates takes place. Candidates are taught to protect themselves; and sometimes make wrong decisions in when to use force, hence, police misconduct in the form of charges or incidents of police brutality. Professionalism, ethics, compassion, empathy, objectivity and cultural awareness issues are not stressed in training, and appear not to be of major concern to some police administrators.

Willingham further states:

Candidates are taught pride and respect for the uniform and demand the same from the community. Police officers believe they should obtain respect, and if necessary, will take corrective action to maintain and avoid losing respect. The information learned while in training and personal experiences on the street affect some officers in a negative way which can lead to police misconduct.

3. OVERWHELMED BY POWER

Many officers are psychologically and emotionally overwhelmed by the immense power and authority that comes with being an officer of the law. Legislators draft the laws of the state, police officers are the *enforcers* of those laws. The power that is inherited with being an officer causes many of them to close the gap between themselves and the law. Hence, many officers see themselves as "the law" instead of agents of the law. Even the mature officer has to check himself on a regular basis to determine if their immense power and authority are corrupting his attitude and behavior.

Policing demands individuals who can function on high psychological and emotional levels. Many officers are barely out of their teens when they join the police department. They are not fully developed emotionally and psychologically. The combination of immense power and authority with underdeveloped character is a formula for serious abuses of power and authority. As the adage goes, power corrupts and absolute power corrupts absolutely.

4. POLICE CULTURE

Any meaningful examination or critique of police officers must go beyond individual officers to exploring the whole culture with which they exist. Police culture is a major variable that generates police misconduct. The police department is America in miniature. American culture is centered on power and control. Consequently, police culture has the same centering.

Police administrations exercise tremendous control over officers—some more than others. Some administrations are insensitive and place high demands on officers. These pressures are frequently vented in the streets in the form of police misconduct, such as rudeness, disrespect, physical abuse, etc.

Rigid departmental regulations and time-consuming demands create stress and tension in police households, leaving many officers emotionally bankrupt. These factors combined with an administration that is highly insensitive to the personal and family needs of officers produce emotional time bombs waiting to explode. No one should be surprised at many of the suicides and homicides by police officers.

A police psychologist who wished to maintain anonymity stated: "The police culture is a sick culture. We take healthy people and make them sick." Many police administrators reject this notion. Instead, they embrace the "rotten apple doctrine." This doctrine says the problem of police misconduct is largely the product of a small number of "rotten apples." The rotten apple doctrine deters meaningful study of the negative impact of police culture on police officers.

5. Harsh Street Experiences

There are individuals who clearly do not have the inner constitution to do police work. However, there are many individuals who appear to be "good" and "well balanced" persons who go through a mental and emotional metamorphosis after receiving a healthy dose of street experience. Street experience can be the seasoning to the aggression inculcated into the officer during the academy. Sergeant Willingham helps us understand how this process occurs. She writes:

> There is usually a rather profound emotional "hardening" of police officers after numerous encounters with the public. Police officers are hardened by the deviousness of the criminal element and often times by "law-abiding" citizens. Victims of crimes are not very happy to see police because they feel it is always after the fact. Citizens become frustrated and sometimes will take out their frustrations on the officer using verbal and/or physical abuse. Police officers become accustomed to the deviousness, and bitterness of the criminal element. Consequently, some police officers become suspicious, cynical, distrustful and skeptical of others.

6. Racism

Despite the stark revelations of the Simpson trial, specifically those regarding White male police misconduct, many people in the larger society still deny that there is a "serious level" of racially motivated misconduct involving

White officers. That whole notion is an insult that African Americans must endure in America. Police departments are microcosms of America. America is racist—police departments are therefore racist. The facts are clear. White male officers comprise the majority of officers in most police departments in America. Internal Affairs Division files throughout the nation are filled with complaints of police misconduct made by Blacks against White male officers.

7. Fear and Anxiety

The inherent danger of police work when combined with the anxiety of working in African American communities, which police departments traditionally label "dangerous" and "high crime," is a big contributor to police misconduct. The fear and anxiety which grip many officers, particularly young White officers who have had little or no association with African Americans, contribute to police abuse in African American communities. These fears create knee-jerk reactions when dealing with verbal and physical confrontations. This helps us understand why there are proportionately higher amounts of police brutality incidents in African American communities.

The subject of misconduct and abuse by Black officers against other Blacks is a difficult one for many Blacks to deal with. However, it is a reality that must be dealt with. The abuse of Blacks by Black officers is the outworking of anxiety and internalized racism. The concept of internalized racism is examined in chapter five, *The Psychology of Gangsterism*. Many Black officers, like other Blacks in America, have a love/hate relationship with Black people.

The frustration of responding to incidents of senseless "Black-on-Black" crime, and crimes involving Black individuals, impacts Black officers in a unique way. When Black officers are on the scene of a tragic "Black-on-Black" violent crime, it generates a brand of frustration White officers simply cannot experience. To the Black officer these are "his people" engaging in nonsensical violence. This unique frustration triggers two very opposite emotional and psychological responses. First, a strong desire to help eradicate the forces that create Black crime and self-annihilation. Second, animosity which leads to the abuse of the people who look just life you.

There is also one additional fact that contributes to the abuse of Black individuals by Black officers. Some Black officers possess such an intense longing for White acceptance that they will abuse other Blacks in order to maintain White acceptance which in many cases is more like tolerance than acceptance.

8. Politics

Politics also contributes to police misconduct. Politicians and police administrators, in their quest to gain or maintain an office, goad law enforcement agencies to produce high arrests. This often translates into poor urban communities being targeted by police. This high intensity policing is occasioned by numerous acts of misconduct which many police administrators and politicians stomach in order to achieve the political benefit of high arrest statistics.

One of the most asked question during the uncovering of Fuhrman's lie regarding his usage of the N-word (nigger) was: How do corrupt police officers, such as Mark Fuhrman, keep from being terminated from the department? Police culture is designed to protect officers from legal, physical and other types of harm. This protection is often provided even when the officer does not fully deserve it.

There are at least 4 reasons corrupt officers and officers who commit serious acts of misconduct are able to maintain employment on the police department. They include: 1) the Blue Wall, 2) supervisor reluctancy to discipline, 3) public acceptance and fear, and 4) complainant credibility.

1. THE BLUE WALL

Police officers maintain a wall of silence around themselves for protection. As Sergeant Willingham explains in her paper, this wall can be difficult to penetrate. She writes:

> The "Blue Wall," which is a conspiracy of silence among police officers, surrounds a police department and is very powerful. The Blue Wall of silence as it is called protects those officers involved in acts of misconduct. No officer wants to be known as someone who reported the actions of his/her fellow officer. There is a much stronger wall, the "Brass Wall." The Brass Wall protects the inner enclave, guarding the reputations and careers of officers; it encourages police misconduct. Officers who report incidents of misconduct are relegated to the worst assignments or forced to resign because of retaliatory pressure from supervisors and/or administrators. The guilty parties are protected and given "cush" jobs which appear on the surface to be a reinforcement or reward for their actions. It would take a strong administrator to break down both walls and expose the actions of the officers and the "Brass" that protects them.

2. SUPERVISOR RELUCTANCY TO DISCIPLINE

Some supervisors are reluctant to address acts of police misconduct. The value system of police officers causes them to minimize the seriousness of many acts of police misconduct. Hence, punishment that is suitable to the act committed by officers is often not meted out. What is interesting is when an officer offends a supervisor, or is wanted out of the department for any number of unjustifiable reasons, it is highly likely that the officer will be discriminately sought out for punishment or termination.

3. PUBLIC ACCEPTANCE AND FEAR

Urban Black communities possess a general acceptance of victimization by police. The view that victimization by police is a part of the whole Black experience discourages filing complaints. Other Blacks do not report victimization by police simply because they fear police retaliation.

4. COMPLAINANT CREDIBILITY

A significant measure of credibility is bestowed the position of police officer. Many investigators of police misconduct are swayed by a complainant's socioeconomic position and personal history. Therefore, the weight of a complaint on a police officer is determined by the complainant's social status. If the complainant is wealthy, prominent, a relative or a close friend of a politician or high-ranking police administrator, his complaint is generally given considerable weight. However, if the complainant lives in a poor section of town, has a serious criminal history, is a known criminal, or is complaining of an incident that occurred during their arrest, the weight of their complaint is generally weak. The exception to this case is a complaint filed against an officer that a supervisor or administration is targeting.

When police administrations in Texas mete out discipline to officers for abuse or misconduct, the decisions are overturned about two-thirds of the time through officer appeals to civil service[32]. Some White investigators of police misconduct are themselves motivated by racism. Hence, when the officer is White, and the complaining person is Black, inconsistencies in that person's complaint are often used to render them without credibility.

The standard recruit personality, police culture, racism, politics and weaknesses in the civil service system create rogue officers who abuse members of the African American community, and preserves these officers, permitting them to continue abusing Black people.

EIGHT

COUNTERING THE SEDUCTION

The seduction machination is real. The criminal justice system does have a history of being more aggressively postured in dealing with Blacks. The structure of urban Black social systems gives crime and violence an alluring appeal. The media and scientific communities have historically engaged in campaigns of smearing the Black image with crime and violence. The use of Black crime and criminalized Black images have long been used by the ruling elite to justify the abuse and economic exploitation of Blacks.

However, whose responsibility is it to terminate these gross processes? It is apparent that many of those participating in them have political and economic incentives to continue. Clearly, it is the responsibility of the African American community to terminate those abuses. Failure to shoulder this responsibility could render the African American community virtually nonexistent in the years to come. In addition to political and economic incentives, the mental eye of Whites in general is blocked by pervasive denial and avoidance. These factors prevent them from confronting the realities of the seduction machination.

Furthermore, denial and avoidance cause many Whites who are involved in the resolution of Black problems to approach them as though Blacks are the singular problem. Whites promote conflict-resolution as though the problem is Black people's inability to handle disputes. They encourage sports as though Blacks engage in crime simply because they are bored. They support introducing Black youth to prominent, successful Blacks as though the problem is they merely do not think they can succeed. These approaches should not be completely discouraged. However, they do not go to the root of many Black problems.

Whites largely ignore social variables that exist because of racism and economic disempowerment. These conditions create frustration and steer youth into crime. We realize society is not 100 percent of the problem, but neither are Blacks.

Many local Black communities have failed to be on the vanguard of resolving their problems. This failure has given government and White social service organizations the opportunity to capitalize on the Black plight. In addition, Blacks have typically accepted low-paying or non-paying positions in these organizations.

Black communities who have failed in this regard have done so for two main reasons. First, many Blacks accept the notion that Blacks are their singular problem. Consequently, they opt not to participate in grass-roots efforts to heal Black ills. Second, the concepts of race-neutrality and color-blindness have made many Blacks oblivious to the realities of racism. Therefore, it does not matter to them who leads this effort. These people can be seen being exploited by White social service organizations who use them to gain political and economic resources.

Many Blacks are confused about the race struggle. This confusion can be attributed largely to the notion of creating a race-neutral and color-blind society. The only problem is Blacks are playing the race-neutral/color-blind game by themselves. While Blacks are playing this game solo, Whites and others are scoring all the points. African Americans are using their degrees and acquired expertise to bring economic and political increase to others, not themselves.

Race-neutrality and color-blindness are traps of political and economic erosion. Some say this is a racist opinion. They tout that America is now a "multicultural society." However, is it really? The 21-member bipartisan body appointed by President George Bush, called the Glass Ceiling Commission reports that almost 97 percent of senior-level managers in the Fortune 1000 industrial and Fortune 500 service industries are White and 0.6 percent are African American. The seats of president and vice-president of the Unites States have only been occupied by White men. A 1995 study conducted by the Southern Education Foundation, called Redeeming the American Promise, reported that while school segregation has been illegal for more than 40 years, most public colleges and universities in the South remain segregated. Let us not forget that many school districts have yet to add African world history to its curriculum.

Multiculturalism is another harmful notion being peddled to the African American community. This concept suggests that African Americans experience problems because they are not being enriched by other cultures. This is sorely untrue. African Americans embrace other cultures. In many ways they embrace aspects of other cultures more than they do their own. Lack of dedication to their culture is a cause of their social and economic deficiencies.

Whites and other non-Blacks benefit from Black people's lack of support to their culture. Blacks provide political and economic support, labor, money and mental energy to other people in the name of "multiculturalism." Consequently, the Black community is dependent upon non-Blacks for political representation, information, social services, jobs, etc. Such dependence is frightening. When a people control your politics, education, news and source of income, they control your lives. The African American community will never become liberated as long as it maintains this reliant relationship upon others.

African Americans must remove what Nathan and Julia Hare call, "The White Liberal/Moderate Choke Hold." This choke hold prohibits Black autonomy (the right to self-government). White liberals and moderates may be well-meaning, but their EuroAmerican upbringing causes to them to unconsciously dominate Blacks. This domination is not mean-spirited, rather it is benevolent—domination with a smile. However, benevolent White domination is as stifling to total Black development as mean-spirited White domination.

White American approaches to resolving Black problems dismiss the peculiarities of Black history. A group's psychology, anatomical structure, social circumstances and plight are the product of their history. These differences demand the application of solutions that deal with the unique characteristics of a group's problems. Whites bring solutions to Black problems that generally oppose their genuine resolution. African Americans require solutions that are adaptable to the unique causes of their plight.

This book recommends a 13-point strategy to attack the unique causes of crime in the African American community, and terminate the other operations of the seduction machination.

1. RESOLVE THE PSYCHIC PAIN OF THE MAAFA

The catastrophic experiences of the Maafa inflicted deep lacerations on the African psyche. The Eurocentric approach to the study of African American oppression is sterile and discounts the agony of its victims. This approach is in harmony with the attitude of Supreme Court Chief Justice Roger B. Taney, who in the famous Dred Scott v. Sanford case wrote: "They

[Africans] had for more than a century before been regarded as beings of an inferior order . . . they had no rights which the White man was bound to respect." Justice Taney did not consider Africans fully human; the Eurocentric approach to the study of African American oppression seems to agree.

The sterile approach of Western history to this subject dampens the deep psychic suffering of these experiences. Racism causes Whites to depreciate Black pain. Whites mourn the loss of their sons and daughters 50 years after their unfortunate death in war. They understand the need for counseling to recover from the trauma of a loved one's death. However, many Whites underrate the pain Blacks felt in watching Alex Haley's *Roots* when it was serialized on television. White devaluation of Black pain caused by cruel and inhumane enslavement is expressed in the commonly made statement: "I'm tired of the Blacks talking about slavery . . . that was a long time ago." Whites even devalue the anguish of recent Jim Crow terrorism. It matters not that African Americans have not been counseled or taken through a psychological reconstruction process.

Enslaved Africans lived with the death of loved ones. They lived with the bitter reality that they could be slaughtered at any minute. African Americans experienced more than a century of Jim Crow violence. Nonetheless, many Whites feel that 25 years of "freedom" is sufficient time to recover from this violent legacy.

African Americans attempt to soothe the pain of oppression by indulging in excessive eating, alcohol, narcotics, sexual promiscuity, conspicuous consumption, etc. Resolving the psychic heritage of the Maafa can help correct these unhealthy behavioral patterns. African Americans who are wounded by oppression have distinct markings. They include the following:

- feeling inferior to Whites
- fearing Whites
- percieving Whites as better than Blacks
- an intense feeling of discomfort with the thought of being self-employed
- having a strong need for a "secure" job
- a strong reliance upon Whites
- feeling that being intelligent is being White
- the desire to be White
- feeling ashamed of your African descendance
- negative attitudes toward Black esthetics, i.e., tight hair, thick lips, dark skin, wide noses, etc.

Psychic healing can occur by taking African Americans back to Africa via movies and documentaries and carrying them through the Maafa so that they may release bitter feelings associated with it. Black radio stations, billboards, fashion designers, television shows, magazines, newspapers, newsletters, community centers, churches and schools should flood the Black community with the Nguzu Saba (Kwanzaa) principles. Umoja—unity; Kujichagulia—self-determination; Ujima—collective work and responsibility; Ujamaa—cooperative economics; Nia—purpose; Kuumba—creativity, and Imani—faith in God, has to become locked into the African American mind.

Special emphasis must be placed on Imani and Ujima. A cultural and psychological rebirth helps resolve the pain associated with the legacy of oppression. However, a spiritual rebirth is even more vital because it connects us to God, who enhances other relationships. Black neighborhoods, organizations, economics, politics, and marriages develop through good relationships. The rifts, breaches and fractures in Black relationships contribute to weaknesses in these areas.

African Americans cannot afford to practice individualism. Subordinated groups help keep themselves in that position when individuals act as autonomous beings or islands unto themselves. Only when a group has control can its members have the benefit of acting somewhat as individuals. The practice of individualism by African Americans only ensures their subordination. The internalization of Nguzu Saba principles into the Black mind will nurture unity, maximize Black strength and promote diversified approaches to liberation.

2. OPTIMAL BLACK CHILD DEVELOPMENT

Optimal intellectual and character development make a person less vulnerable to negative variables that draw them into crime. Black parents, teachers, and other child care givers must learn the skill of maximizing the intellect and character of Black children. We must ask ourselves: When Blacks permit non-Blacks to determine whether their children can be taught, what they are taught, where they are taught, and who teaches them, can Black children be maximally developed?

Educational systems work best for those who design them. Black children are not maximally developed in American educational systems because they were designed by Whites for Whites; therefore, they are not suitable to Black psychology. This does not suggest that it is impossible for Blacks to excel in American educational systems. Many Blacks have excelled in White-controlled educational systems. This speaks to the strength and ability of Black children.

The principal responsibility of educating Black children rests upon Blacks. Many Blacks felt that "integrated" schools would bring fairness to America's prejudiced educational system. Consequently, they began agitating for integrated classrooms. In the mid-'60s, Black parents and the NAACP in Boston, Massachusetts met with the all-White Boston School

Committee chaired by Louise Day Hicks. They wanted the committee to address the racial imbalance of Boston public schools. However, Ms. Hicks and the school committee refused to honor their request, claiming that there were no problems with the current school structure.

Despite the 1954 Brown v. Board of Education ruling by the Supreme Court, and a state law banning racially imbalanced schools, Blacks had to take their struggle to the federal level. In June 1974, a federal judge ruled that the Boston School Board consciously maintained two school districts — one Black, one White. The judges' solution to this problem was forced busing. Whites refused to honor the federal court order. When school opened, more than 50 percent of White students were kept home. The buses that carried Blacks to the White schools were pelted with rocks, and the students were verbally assaulted as they walked into the schools. Tension was high in the school building. Blacks and Whites engaged in numerous fights[33].

Integration weakened the Black community. Their schools were closed, teachers were terminated, principals were demoted, and children were miseducated. Many Blacks question whether integration was good strategy. In an essay in *The Isis Papers* entitled *Black Children and the Process of Inferiorization*, Dr. Welsing writes:

> Black children are our most valuable possession and our greatest potential resource. Any meaningful discussion of the survival or the future of Black people must be predicated upon Black people's plan for the maximal development of all Black children. If the children's lives are squandered, and if the children of a people are not fully developed at whatever cost and sacrifice, the people will have consigned themselves to certain death.

Black survival is dependent upon Black children reaching full development. What are Blacks doing to ensure their survival? The development of Black children cannot rest in the hands of fate. There must be a plan. But in order for this plan to work, Black parents must raise their expectations of their children. The August 5, 1991 issue of *Newsweek* magazine contained the results of a survey conducted by The Metropolitan Chicago Information Center. It revealed that nearly 14 percent of Black adults in the Chicago area agreed that African Americans have less "inborn ability to learn than Whites."

Black parents and child care givers must realize the marvelous intellectual ability of their children. In *Awakening the Natural Genius of Black Children*, Dr. Amos Wilson shows the results of Geber's comparative study of African and European psychomotor development. The results of this study are as follows:

110

COMPARISON OF AFRICAN AND
EUROPEAN PSYCHOMOTOR DEVELOPMENT

- Nine (9) hours old being drawn up in a sitting position, able to prevent its head from falling backward; the European child takes six (6) weeks.

- Two (2) days old, with head held firmly, looking in the face of the examiner; the European child takes eight (8) weeks.

- Seven (7) weeks old, supporting herself in a sitting position and her reflection in the mirror; the European child takes twenty (20) weeks.

- Five (5) months old, holding herself upright; the European child takes nine (9) months.

- Five (5) months old, taking the round block out of its hole in the form board; the European child takes eleven (11) months.

- Five (5) months old, standing against the mirror; the European child takes nine (9) months.

- Seven (7) months old, walking to the Gesell Box to look inside; the European child takes fifteen (15) months.

- Eleven (11) months old, climbing the steps alone; the European child takes fifteen (15) months.

This study demonstrates that African children are born with a natural head start. Many Black parents fail to take advantage of this natural "head start." Black parents tend to rely totally upon schools to educate their children. They should become proficient in fundamental tools that will develop their child's intellectual abilities. Listed below are eight simple and effective "learning to learn skills" parents can practice every day that will send their child on the way to optimal intellectual development. They include:

- paying attention
- self-control
- persistence
- completing tasks
- observance
- curiosity
- obedience to rightful authority
- joy of learning

111

Black children who have been educated in African-centered educational settings have outperformed so-called gifted and talented White students in grades higher than them. The Marcus Garvey School in Los Angeles teaches two-year-old students to recite the names of all the major bones in Latin, name all 50 states, and recite the alphabet in three languages.

The EuroAmerican method of educating Black children limits Black intellectual development. Blacks are therefore paralyzed by their dependence on public schools. Black people must establish African-centered child development centers and schools. The alternative is to gain control of local schools and staff them with teachers and administrators committed to teaching Black students. Black men must also enter the field of education. The male influence is essential to optimal child development.

Blacks must create a culture that breeds business owners, not merely managers and law-makers, not just law-abiders. Blacks therefore must place greater emphasis on "intellectual athletics" than on physical athletics and entertainment. This does not mean that sports and the arts are void of value. They serve a vital function in the development of discipline, character and team skills. However, our future is bleak when significant numbers of Black students see professional athletics and entertainment as their only career prospect.

Black children cannot be permitted to speak Black English alone. They must master the English language and learn other languages as well. Black children must become proficient in writing, math, science and computer skills. Black parents must cultivate a love for reading and computers within their children. This can be done by reading with them on a regular basis and buying a home computer. Parents must also monitor the time and programs children watch on television. And it is important to understand that parents are not their children's buddy.

The high percentage of single-female parents raises certain vitally important issues. In *Countering the Conspiracy to Destroy Black Boys*, Dr. Jawanza Kunjufu raises one of those issues. Kunjufu discusses how some mothers "love their sons and raise their daughters." Why do some mothers love their sons and raise their daughters? They do so because for many single-female parents their son(s) serve as emotional substitutes for a husband. But when single mothers are more lenient with their sons than their daughters, their sons often suffer with underdeveloped character.

Parents must not deride one another in front of their children. Children must have a healthy image of the mother and father role. The best environment for a child is a two-parent household. Each sex possesses certain essential qualities a child needs to achieve healthy development. This means divorced and uncommitted parents must do their best to maintain a workable relationship so that both can provide their children's emotional and psychological needs.

Failing to discipline children is a form of hate. Discipline is an essential ingredient to success in life. Disciplining children is therefore a high expression of parental love. Parents set their children up to fail when they do not discipline them. It is important to emphasise that parents should guard against being impulsive in disciplining their children. Discipline must be consistent, balanced and goal-oriented. This kind of discipline produces children who are consistent, well-balanced and focused.

Parents should engage in constant self-development. What children need more than any "thing" in this world is a mature parent. Adequate parenting will also help terminate the deadly phenomenon of teenage parents.

3. THE BLACK RELIGIOUS COMMUNITY

Black churches play a key role in terminating the seduction machination. The church is God's channel of power, but it has largely failed to fully demonstrate this power with regard to the plight of Black people. However, there is good news. A concept called Liberation Theology is being embraced by many churches throughout the country. Liberation Theology is a relevant and practical message that deals with the spiritual, social, psychological, political and economic needs of Black people. The Bible does not instruct Christians to avoid "the world." On the contrary, numerous directives are given to Christians that instruct them to reach out to those in the world. Isaiah 61:1-3 reads:

> The Spirit of the Lord is on me, because he hath anointed me to preach good news to the *poor*. He has sent me to bind up the *brokenhearted*, to proclaim freedom for the *captives* and release for the *prisoners*.

The Ten Point Coalition in Boston, Massachusetts is Liberation Theology in action. This organization comprises more than twenty churches that work together under a ten-point, labor-intensive agenda. This agenda entails:

- adopting gangs
- court advocation
- youth evangelism
- economic development
- linking churches
- neighborhood crime watch
- decentralized health services
- Christian brotherhood summits
- rape crisis centers
- Black history curriculums[34]

113

The church must reach out to incarcerates with jail and prison ministries. The concept of adopting a prisoner can develop relationships that foster lasting rehabilitation. Black religious organizations must encourage Black entrepreneurship. The Bible promises believers wealth and property ownership. Our high goal should not be limited to merely managing the wealth and property of others. Observe these excerpts from Deuteronomy chapter 28 verses 4,5,8 and 12:

> Blessed shall be the fruit of *thy* ground, and the fruit of *thy* cattle . . . Blessed shall be *thy* basket and *thy* store . . . The lord shall command the blessing upon thee in *thy* storehouses . . . Thou shalt lend to many nations, and thou shalt not borrow.

Black religious organizations must add the practical to the spiritual. They should serve as training stations for starting and developing businesses. Black religious organizations possess a wealth of business knowledge and experience that can be tapped and used to lead people as safely as possible into establishing their own enterprises. The Allen A.M.E. Church in New York City serves as a national model for churches spurring Black economic empowerment. It purchased more than 15 vacant storefronts in Queens, New York and opened a barber shop, restaurant, medical and legal office, travel agency and preschool[35].

Black religious organizations must begin an aggressive campaign to correctly redefine Black manhood. Nation of Islam leader Minister Louis Farrakhan possesses great skills in attracting Black men. He and his men project a strong male image. Black men are attracted to the respect for Black manhood the Muslim men demand. Minister Farrakhan was able to attract thousands of Black men throughout the nation to "For Men Only" meetings to begin redefining Black manhood. These meetings culminated with the historic Million Man March, with over one million Black men in attendance.

Many Black men view being a Christian synonymous with being weak. Dr. Frank Reid, pastor of Bethel A.M.E Church in Baltimore, Maryland, is erasing that image. He has learned that Black men are drawn by respect. His church has a program for the men of Bethel called "Mighty Men of God." It revives Black manhood through physical discipline, devotion to God and personal development[36].

Black religious organizations must invest in future manhood and womanhood as well. Rites of passage programs for children, and parental skills training will give birth to strong Black communities. The rites of passage and parental skills development models shown below present the basic components of these programs. Be mindful that these models can be tailored to fit the specific needs of your groups.

RITES OF PASSAGE MODEL

PERSONAL - SELF DISCIPLINE, RESPONSIBILITY FOR INDIVIDUAL ACTIONS
- build relationships between youth and elderly
- develop hobbies, i.e., sports, music, computers, speaking, writing
- tell stories and read books on a variety of subjects
- take trips out of the city

SPIRITUAL - FAITH IN GOD
- practice spiritual disciplines, i.e., Bible study, prayer and praise
- compile a list of things to be thankful for

ECONOMIC - SAVINGS AND MONEY MANAGEMENT
- introduce youth to local business persons
- cultivate the entrepreneurial spirit through small businesses operation
- teach money management—bills, credit, taxes, bank accounts
- have youth maintain a budget
- take tours of financial institutions

PHYSICAL - PROPER CARE FOR THE BODY
- take tour of hospitals
- educate on personal hygiene maintenance
- teach sex education
- instruct on the proper care for the body—rest, relaxation and healthy diet

EMOTIONAL - DEVELOPING CONTROL
- talk about the wide variety of emotions—anger, sadness, bitterness, hate, etc.
- teach the art of effective communication—talking and listening
- discuss healthy ways to relieve stress and tension

POLITICAL/SOCIAL - DEVELOPING CONSCIOUSNESS
- have regular discuss social events—local, state, national and global
- introduce youth to politicians
- encourage involvement in school politics
- organize youth groups to address community problems
- discuss the importance of family and community relationships

MENTAL - HIGH INTELLECTUAL ACHIEVEMENT
- design challenging reading programs
- develop programs to develop writing skills
- utilize educational puzzles and games
- insist upon the proper usage of the English language

CULTURAL/HISTORICAL - SELF DEVELOPMENT

- teach African world history
- instruction in the history of other people
- build a family tree
- have historians speak on diverse history subjects

PARENTAL SKILLS DEVELOPMENT MODEL

- teach proper prenatal care
- instruction on the forms of child discipline—emphasis placed on needs v. wants
- discuss effective parent/child communication skills
- educate on the proper care of a child's health
- share effective keys to language development
- instruct on how to develop children's intellectual skills
- teach how to develop a child's behavior

Spiritual settings offer the best environment for rites of passage training. People's lives are optimally impacted when their heart and spirit are touched. Black religious organizations must address drug addiction through substance abuse programs. They must encourage their children to maintain educational excellence. This can be accomplished through academic achievement celebrations and scholarship awards to college students. Denominational walls must be torn down in order to maximize the potential of the Black religious community. The formation of an interdenominational and interfaith alliance could bring needed structure and organization to this mission.

4. A BLACK AMERICAN ECONOMIC SYSTEM

A malfunctioning economic system makes a community vulnerable to social pressures; consequently, people in that community become less able to resist the lure of crime. When money only flows out of a community, it will become instable and plummet into disorder. The disorder of many Black communities can be attributed to money not flowing into their economic systems. The reason money does not flow into local Black economic systems is not because all Blacks are poor. Black America's annual income is more than 350 billion dollars. This qualifies Black America to be the ninth richest nation in the world.

One of the reasons money does not flow into the Black American community is that Blacks do not think of themselves as a nation within a nation. This may be the United States of America, but it is not the United Races of America. America is a compilation of people who function as nations. Every race in America acts as a nation within this nation except

Blacks. Consequently, Blacks give their money to other nations as their nation deteriorates.

Nation building cannot take place without building a strong economic system. It is not enough to have thousands of African Americans with high five, six, and seven figure incomes. That income must serve to build an African American economic system. Blacks take jobs away from themselves, send Black businesses into bankruptcy and prevent the growth of new business by giving their money to non-Blacks. Many Blacks have fallen for the ruse of economic color-blindness.

Blacks must develop an alternative source of acquiring capital for business development other than banks. Banks have historically been apprehensive about lending money to Blacks for entrepreneurial ventures despite the fact that they grow through using Black dollars. The Asians have demonstrated that the Kwanzaa principle of Ujamaa—cooperative economics—can build large pools of capital. Blacks must use money to build wealth, not simply to acquire symbols of wealth.

5. BLACK CONSUMERS

The Black consumer's role in the systemization of Black economics is paramount. Blacks must purge their minds of those economically disempowering philosophies of race-neutrality and color-blindness. Blacks spend a mere three cents of every dollar they earn with Blacks. This means 97 cents of every Black dollar goes to other people. This demonstrates that the concept of color-blindness does not need to be encouraged in the Black community, but the concept of seeing Black does.

6. LOCAL BLACK COMMUNITIES

Local Black communities need a revival of the extended family concept. This concept fortifies the bonds of unity that strengthen Black communities to endure harsh oppression. The Eurocentric value of individualism leveled the extended family structure in many parts of the Black community. Black communities then became weak and disorganized, which triggered the disintegration process. Three decades ago, child rearing was the work of the community. Mrs. Brown next door did not hesitate to chasten you when you misbehaved. Today some Black parents resent other adults for scolding their children. The principle of Ujima—collective work and responsibility— must come into practice. Collective work and responsibility provides Black communities the needed protection and power to overcome their plight. The Montgomery Bus Boycott is an example of the power of collective work.

Local Black communities can effect change through organizing groups who lobby on behalf of the entire Black community, engage in political activism, picket, boycott and conduct letter-writing campaigns. They can utilize neighborhood organizations as investment groups and use monies collected in dues to purchase dilapidated structures in their neighborhood for organizational use or to sell them to responsible buyers. They must protect their economic and legal interests with vigilance. They must engage in watch-dogging for civil rights violations, excessive uses of force and unnecessary uses of deadly force by members of the justice system. The Black community cannot afford to have its members unjustifiably arrested, over-sentenced and murdered under color of law. It must also take a strong and definite stand against "Black-on-Black" crime.

The subject of police brutality is a major concern to urban Black communities. There are two strategies Blacks can utilize to combat this activity. The first strategy is proactive. It involves standing a reasonable distance away from officers who are dealing with suspects on the street. The impact of George Holliday's videotaping of the Rodney King beating was substantial on police misconduct. After this incident, most officers exercised extra care in handling individuals on the street. They were concerned that "electronic eyes" might catch them engaging in misconduct. Officers were even concerned about the appearance of misconduct.

The second strategy is reactive. It involves strategies to counter police misconduct. Many people who feel they were mishandled by police fail to complain because they feel they cannot win or fear retaliation. Complaints must be tailored to fit the temperament of a police department's administrative staff. When an administrative staff is arrogant and insensitive it is generally seen in the officers. Conversely, when an administrative staff is concerned about fairness it tilts the scales toward fairness in the streets. Therefore, a wave of detailed complaints of police misconduct may be sufficient to evoke a genuine response by some police departments. However, in less sensitive departments, it may require a wave of detailed complaints, law suits filed, and mass protests to force that administration into action.

7. COLLABORATION BETWEEN THE LEGAL SYSTEM AND THE BLACK COMMUNITY

The criminal justice community, law enforcement in particular, have long been "marionettes of the elite." The elite have used law enforcement to regulate Black movement and progress in America. However, the concept of community policing does offer a ray of hope for Black communities. This concept is transforming police officers to peace officers. It is transforming police work in the African American community to service instead of force. However, we should not let the boasts of law enforcement professionals concerning the successes of community policing confuse us. Police departments still need vast improvements.

One area where improvement is still needed is the relationship the criminal justice community has with the Black community. This is crucial because there must be collaboration between the legal system and the African American community if adequate crime prevention, maximally effective and fair justice, and the neutralization of crime and violence are to be realized in the African American community. However, in order to achieve maximal collaboration between the criminal justice and Black communities, the criminal justice system must confront the issue of its injustice. These are some of the measures that must be taken to facilitate this:

- All racial and socioeconomic subgroups must be equally held accountable to the law.

- Every dimension of the justice system must be assertive, but fair, with regard to the collective African American community.

- All sectors of the justice system must have adequate African American representation. This includes all ranks of the police system, prosecuting and defense lawyers, judges, all levels of the prison system, probation and parole officers.

- Personnel in the justice system must shed negative stereotypes of Blacks and Black communities. A thorough knowledge of the history, culture and experiences of African Americans can help break down these stereotypes.

- Police departments must deal forthrightly with the general "Rambo attitude" police officers possess.

- African Americans in the justice system must become Africentered in their consciousness. They should not disconnect and dissociate themselves from African Americans in the lower socioeconomic echelon.

- Any act of discrimination, civil rights violation, or abuse of Black people by any member of the justice system must be handled in a timely fashion. Offenders must be given swift and appropriate disciplinary actions.
- Police administrations must put forth every effort to prevent officers from trampling upon the rights of the law abiding in order to deal with crime.

- The African American community must be prepared to address any individual or group, i.e., offenders, police officers, attorneys, judges, prison staffers who mistreat, abuse or harm in any way members of its community. When such offenses occur, African Americans must follow through to ensure that these offenders, regardless of color, are handled in a timely and judicious manner.

8. BLACK LEADERSHIP AND CIVIL RIGHTS ORGANIZATIONS

Black leadership and civil rights organization have been weakened by their disunity and lack of diversified approaches to solving Black problems. These weaknesses disempower Blacks. They are the reasons Blacks have been limited to addressing civil rights issues. The Black protest movement of the '50s and '60s stood on a heavy civil rights platform. The overt violation of Black people's civil rights made that approach appropriate in that day. However, in the '90s racism is not the only issue threatening the future of the African American community. Economic matters pose serious threats to the collective African American community. Economic development and empowerment must be main issues on the Black American agenda to ensure a healthy future.

Until recently, Black economics had not been given the adequate attention it demands. Black leadership bears some of the responsibility for this. They have traditionally been a ministerial leadership. Their approaches to solving Black problems have been influenced by biblical principles of "love" and "loving your enemy." This has caused them to see the creation of a loving, racially harmonious society as a main solution to the Black plight. Consequently, Black strategy was centered heavily on "assimilation tactics." The issue of Black economic empowerment, which should not be mistaken for high Black employment, was not given consistent attention.

This leadership has also failed to "pass the baton" to up-and-coming leaders, thus discouraging diversity in approaches to dealing with Black problems. However, young adults also bear some responsibility for this. They must take a position on the platform of Black leadership. Young Blacks must establish new organizations and engage in activism that gives the old regime reason to "pass the baton."

As stated earlier, the lack of unity in Black leadership has impeded the progress of the collective Black community. Black leaders and organizations simply must check their egos and minor differences at the door and coalesce. They must go into the planning room and design strategies and tactics to build African American social, political and economic power. They must design strategies to counter the seduction machination, which entails the criminalization of the Black image, the abuse of Blacks by the justice system in the name of a "war on crime" and "a war on drugs," and the construction of a revised Jim Crow society justified by Black crime and their frightening images.

According to the Philadelphia-based research group, Motivational

Education Entertainment, 97 percent of Black youth between 12 and 20 enjoy rap music. Black leaders can collaborate with members of the music industry to communicate to younger African Americans and create greater interest in the liberation movement. Ice Cube, Chuck D, KRS-One (Kris Parker), Arrested Development (Speech), Queen Latifah (Dana Owens), and others could be most useful in initiating such a collaborative endeavor.

Many Black leaders and organizations are bankrolled by White corporations. Many of these corporations peddle products that harm Blacks. According to the Centers for Disease Control, cigarettes killed nearly 48,000 African Americans in 1988. Can Black progress only be attained through tolerating the demise of thousands of Blacks due to cigarettes and alcohol?

The financial support of Black organizations by Black people is vital to Black self-government. Black leadership can then take the power vested in them by the people and use it to its fullest potential. Black political power can be maximized by Blacks becoming the nation's swing vote. The Democratic party's lack of interfacing with the Black community is evidence that it takes the Black vote for granted. And the Republican party's political reality is one that will bring about political, economic and social regression in sections of the Black community. Being the swing vote forces both parties to take Blacks more seriously.

Political participation backed by economic power is important. Remember Reconstruction? There were tremendous gains made in law enforcement, civil rights and politics between 1860 and 1870. However, in the 1870s Blacks saw their gains rolled back in their faces, and a new version of the old slavery created. We must vote.

9. STATISTICAL COMPILATION AND ANALYSIS OF BLACK ISSUES FOR EFFECTIVE DEBATE

Politics to a large extent is a war of words. The African American community must utilize trained researchers to compile information regarding Black economics, crime, violence, family, education, health, employment, and other issues, to arm itself for the verbal war. It must also cultivate and utilize debaters who can effectively engage in this war to counter the myth and misinformation promoted about the African American community through misleading statistics, media and pseudo-science.

African Americans should conduct studies on matters pertaining to themselves. The information obtained in studies and statistical compilation should be accessible to the general African American community. It can use this information to counter misleading statistical sources such as the UCR, and false studies such as *The Bell Curve*.

10. BLACK CRIMINAL JUSTICE PROFESSIONALS

Black criminal justice professionals should serve as roadblocks of injustice. This demands a tremendous amount of courage and commitment. Many

Blacks are not aware of how beneficial it is to have dedicated Blacks in criminal justice. If there were no dedicated Blacks in criminal justice, the tribulations of Blacks going through the criminal justice process would be much worse.

Black criminal justice professionals experience tremendous frustration. They are not immune from Dubois' double consciousness. Many are torn between Blackness and Whiteness. Some opt to enjoy the "repossessable benefits" of limited White acceptance, which come by identification and conformation. This duality often leads Blacks in criminal justice to abuse and mistreat Blacks. These Blacks must also guard against appearing to be "too Black." However, other Blacks in this field opt not to conform to the standard set by the majority group. They are often labeled radical and are perceived as traitors. They do not turn away or hesitate to speak up when injustices are committed in the name of justice. Such behavior comes with a price.

Judge Bruce Wright's book entitled *Black Robes, White Justice*, addresses this matter as it relates to Black judges. The judge writes:

> There are black judges who are so godly in their dark ascendance, so remote in the social distance they imagine separates them from their kith and kin of melanin, that they joyously believe themselves to be charter members of the black bourgeoisie. Status-conscious imposters by self-anointment, they are so white in their imitation of life and in their reactions to black defendants that they are known as "Afro-Saxons."

Wright further states:

> They are black judges in skin color only. They fail to understand that if there is no difference between white and black judges, there is no need to emphasize the paucity of black judges or the deliberate exclusion of black lawyers from the bench through the use of limiting quotas.

Black police officers are a dire necessity in the streets of the Black community. They generally bring a perspective and an attitude in dealing with Blacks that Whites cannot. White officers can be effective servants in the Black community. However, it is difficult for most Whites to shed from their minds the negative images of Blacks, particularly urban Blacks, that are embedded deep within the American mind. Moreover, Whites have enjoyed social dominance for centuries. It is difficult for them to loose their egos from the mental strings of dominant group position. These factors cause many White officers to approach policing in the Black community with a "hunter/dictator mentality."

The presence of Black officers serve as a defense against other officers mistreating Blacks in the streets, or in the station. White officers who would normally hurl racist remarks at Blacks, or take a few strikes at them with their baton, generally restrain themselves from such behavior in the presence of socially and politically conscious Black officers.

Black attorneys have an awesome responsibility in the criminal justice process. Whether defender or prosecutor, it must be their goal to counter the inequities of criminal investigative and judicial processes. Most law schools do not devote meaningful time to the study of law for the underprivileged. They are devoted to the study of law for the privileged. This approach produces lawyers who have little or no interest in the injustices dealt poor and non-White people.

The discretion judges have in sentencing is another matter that must be addressed to stop courtroom discrimination. State judges in particular possess a tremendous amount of discretion in sentencing offenders. In the state of Texas, a first degree felony is punishable from 5 to 99 years, with a fine of up to $10,000[37]. This wide range of punishment provides judges with ample room to discriminate in sentencing.

Federal Judge Marvin Frankel expressed concern for the problem of sentencing is the judicial system. In his book entitled *Criminal Sentences* he writes:

> The sentencing powers of the judges are, in short, so far unconfined that, except for frequently monstrous maximum limits, they are effectively subject to no law at all.

Judges could be given sentencing guidelines that will bring consistency of sentencing to offenders of all socioeconomic classes and races. Black criminologists must be more visible and vocal with regard to all the critical issues surrounding Black criminality. There are a number of Black criminologists in America who could be most useful in a national initiative to neutralize crime in the Black community.

11. BLACK ENTERTAINERS AND ENTERTAINMENT EXECUTIVES

Blacks in the television, motion picture and record industries have at their disposal the power of words and images. They can utilize their power in two ways. First, they can further damage the Black image by projecting powerful words and images which romanticize crime and violence. Second, they can use their position to repair the damaged Black image and project images of value and power.

In order to accomplish this, Blacks in this industry should form their own television networks, production companies and open their own studios. This may not happen anytime soon, but in the meanwhile, when Black entertainers are given input in shaping Black characters, they should do their best to ensure that the Black image is not negatively one-dimensional.

Black America must fully support Blacks in these industries who maintain their artistic integrity. They must also be prepared to discipline those in this field who themselves have been seduced into engaging in the degrading process of negative Black image projection. We should be prepared to refrain from watching the programs, attending the shows, listening to the radio stations, and buying the records of those who engage in criminalizing the Black image.

The African American community needs movies that are not Blaxploitative in nature. Ghetto dramas can definitely serve a vital educational function. However, it is important that we see the projection of images in motion pictures, television programs and videos that portray Blacks in pursuit of educational excellence, involved in successful entrepreneurial ventures, and engaging in healthy relationships. Social despair, conflict in relationships and tragedy are realities in the Black community, but they are not the total reality of the Black American experience.

We must maximize the benefits of our financial contribution to these industries. Blacks purchase nearly 40 percent of records sold[38]. Black artists rake in millions of dollars through album sales and concert performances. However, the collective African American economy receives little financial benefit in relation to the amount of money and talent it supplies this industry. Blacks purchase 40 percent of movie tickets sold[39]. They should possess greater power and control over this industry opposed to being high-paid employees. There should also be movie theaters in Black communities.

Blacks supply a significant amount of production and business ingenuity to these industries as well. They include: Andre Harrell/Motown Records, Sean Combs/Bad Boys Entertainment, Quincy Jones/Quest Records, Queen Latifah/Flavor Unit, Antonio Reid and Kenneth Edmonds/LaFace Records, Russell Simmons/Def Jam Records, and a host of musicians and vocal artists.

Black artistic talent and business expertise places a stout amount of money into the bank accounts of the highest executive echelon of this industry. LaFace Records is a $37 million business. The label that launched LaFace makes a considerable amount more. With the talent Reid and Edmonds possess, they should control their whole operation.

The Recording Industry Association of America, located in Washington, D.C., reports that the music industry earned $10 billion in 1994. The breakdown by music category is as follows:

•	Rock	**32.0%**
•	Country	**7.5%**
•	Urban Contemporary, Soul, R&B, Dance, Disco,Funk, Fusion and Reggae	**9.9%**

- Rap   **7.8%**
- Jazz   **3.3%**
- Gospel   **3.1%**

Traditional and contemporary Black music earned 24 percent, or nearly $2.5 billion, of the total $10 billion earned. However, Black people are not involved in the more lucrative aspects of the industry, which include packaging, distribution, production and marketing.

With the talents and expertise Blacks in television and motion pictures possess, it is illogical that we do not have more stock in these industries. The list of African American executives, filmmakers, television producers, directors, studio and network owners includes: Oprah Winfrey/Harpo Productions, Robert L. Johnson/Black Entertainment Television, Bill Cosby/ The Cosby Show, Debbie Allen/A Different World, Michael Maye/Married With Children, Jennifer Lawson/Public Broadcasting Service, Spike Lee/ 40 Acres and a Mule Productions, John Singleton/New Deal Productions, Bill Duke/Yagya Productions, Reginald and Warrington Hudlin/Hudlin Brothers Inc., Allen and Albert Hughes, Eddie Murphy/Eddie Murphy Productions, and others.

The supply of business acumen and artistic talent Blacks provide the movie and television industries generate billions of dollars for its all-White upper executive echelon. These companies make phenomenal amounts of money if they can pay actors 50 and 60 million dollars per movie.

Spike Lee, John Singleton, Bill Cosby, Oprah Winfrey and Robert L. Johnson are examples of what Blacks can do in this industry if they work under a collective work principle. Spike's second movie, *She's Gotta Have It*, was made on personal loans and credit card charges amounting to $175,000. Now, Forty Acres and a Mule is a multi-million dollar movie company. John Singleton's Oscar Nomination for *Boyz N The Hood*, which incidentally made more than $60 million, made him the youngest African American filmmaker to win a nomination. *The Cosby Show* lifted NBC from third to first place in television network ratings. Cosby at one time attempted to purchase NBC. Oprah Winfrey owns her own studio in Chicago called Harpo Productions which produces *The Oprah Winfrey Show*. It grossed $180 million in 1993. In fifteen years Robert L. Johnson has garnered more than 10 million subscribers for his satellite cable network Black Entertainment Television[40]. The abilities, talents and potential of Blacks in this industry clearly are astonishing!

Then there is the sports industry. Blacks in this industry, particularly football and basketball, could start their own franchises as Black baseball players once did. The immense wealth being generated by sports could then benefit the African American economic system much more than it currently does. Isaiah Thomas should be commended for taking the basketball franchise knowledge and money he acquired in the NBA and employing it in a basketball franchise. Although it's in Canada, the African American community can benefit from it.

The Bureau of Labor Statistics reports that of the 71,000 people employed as athletes, 10 percent are Black. However, the actual breakdown of the three major sports Blacks are involved in is higher. Blacks represent more than 15 percent of major league baseball players; 60 percent of NFL football players; and 75 percent of NBA basketball players. Annual attendance at these games is high. Baseball attracts 58 million spectators per year; football brings in 18 million per year; and basketball entertains 18 million in yearly attendance. With individual tickets ranging from $15 to $150 per game, the amount of money these sports earn a year runs into the billions.

Blacks in these industries must maintain their artistic integrity and commitment to Black culture and utilize their talents, acquired expertise and financial resources to go from being high-paid employees to owning their own operations. The collective African American community would then benefit far more than it currently does.

12. BLACK JOURNALISTS

Black news media professionals are of invaluable worth to the African American community. They can help dispel the myths surrounding drug abuse and crime in the African American community. African Americans have worked in the mainstream media for more than 50 years. However, most of them feel that conditions for them are not good.

It requires a tremendous amount of courage to be a socially and politically conscious Black journalist. The National Association of Black Journalists conducted a study on journalism in America called *Muted Voices*. Its purpose was to determine if Black journalists felt any apprehensions in dealing with race matters. The survey indicated that one-third of Black journalists were apprehensive about bringing up race issues.

The Black community needs Black journalists who will boldly and accurately write on issues that affect Black people. It needs those who will counter the mythology, stereotypes, bias and misinformation that come from their counterparts. Managerial insensitivity in the newsroom is largely the reason the focus of news coverage in the African American community is on crime, violence, tragedy and controversy. It is also part of the reason Black crime is sensationalized. Managerial insensitivity and the inadequate representation of Black reporters and managers in newsrooms throughout the country result in the low-priority given to meaningful race matters, particularly those that pertain to Blacks, such as the Million Man March.

The Black community must support progressive Black journalists in the mainstream media by putting pressure to bear on managers through the power of the pen and the dollar. If managers do not ensure that Blacks are accurately portrayed in their newspapers and news shows, Blacks should stop buying their publications and supporting their sponsors. The Black community must also support Black newspapers and magazines, especially those that deal with hard-hitting Black issues.

13. AFFLUENT BLACK AMERICANS

Blacks must face the fact that America is a capitalistic society. Therefore, capital is necessary to push a movement. Collective African American progress rests upon money-power as well as man-power. The African American community needs funding to start and maintain various political activities, social services and stimulate economic empowerment. Funding is especially needed to establish Africentric schools so Black children can be educated in high technology, maintain historically Black colleges and universities, finance entrepreneurial ventures, support Black politicians committed to Black people, create various study institutes, and support civil rights organizations.

Bill Cosby, Oprah Winfrey and Michael Jordan have shared a tremendous amount of their wealth with the African American community. They should be highly commended for their immense generosity. However, Mr. Cosby, Ms. Winfrey and Mr. Jordan cannot shoulder this responsibility alone. Every Black person who has been fortunate to acquire great wealth in this country must realize that with the acquisition of wealth comes "the obligation of reciprocation."

Affluent Blacks should endeavor to share their success with their people. It is disheartening when affluent Blacks, who oftentimes are supported by Blacks, spend money to build ultra-lavish houses, purchase luxurious vehicles and throw exorbitant parties and fail to share money, time or their name to uplift Black people. An annual contribution of two to five percent of the annual income of all Black millionaires, combined with the financial contributions of other Blacks, could bankroll a momentous national Black liberation project.

Until this occurs, conscious affluent Blacks should provide financial support to build and support Africentric schools, maintain historically Black colleges and universities, send Black students to college, back civil rights organizations and Black nonprofit social service programs that are effectively addressing Black problems. They could establish financial institutions by which African Americans can access loans to open new businesses or acquire capital for existing businesses in danger of closing. Affluent Blacks can establish philanthropic organizations for African Americans to access grants for meaningful projects.

Countering the seduction is not the responsibility of one particular segment of the Black community, it is the responsibility of the entire Black community. This book asserts that racism is a root cause of Black crime and violence. However, the likely permanence of racism disallows Blacks to work exclusively on the eradication of racism as a main solution to solving crime and violence. The Black community must organize and position itself in such a manner that it is empowered to defend itself against attacks of racism. It is important for Black parents, teachers, school administrators, ministers, parishioners, consumers, business owners, neighborhoods, social service groups, politicians, leaders, leading organizations, police officers, lawyers, judges, probation officers, parole officers, prison workers, entertainers, athletes, journalists and affluents to be dedicated to building a strong and progressive culture that lifts the collective Black community to positions of power and authority. Together we will win!

REFERENCES

LIES AND HALF TRUTHS ABOUT CRIME IN THE BLACK COMMUNITY

1. —,"NAACP Condemns Racist Remarks by Comedian," *Dallas Weekly*, 03/30- 04/05/94.
2. Chideya, Farai, *Don't Beleve the Hype: Fighting Cultural Misinforma tion about African Americans*, New York: Penguine Books Ltd, 1995.
3. —,"Blacks Take Brunt of War on Drugs," *Los Angeles Times*, 04/22/90.
4. Hacker, Andrew, *Two Nations: Black and White, Separate, Hostile, Unequal*, New York: Maxwell Macmillan International, 1992.

WHITE DOMINATION, BLACK CRIMINALITY

5. —,"Boston: A Deadly Family Affair," *Newsweek*, 01/15/90.
6. —,"Tears of Hate, Tears of Pity," *People Weekly*, 03/13/95.
7. Clarke, John Henrik, *Notes for an African World Revolution*, Trenton: African World Press, 1993.

OPPRESSIVE STRATEGIES THAT SEDUCE BLACKS INTO CRIME

8. Rogers, J.A., *The Ku Klux Spirit*, Baltimore: Black Classic Press, 1980.
9. Hutchinson, Earl Ofari, *The Mugging of Black America*, Chicago: African American Images, 1990.
10. Ginzburg, Ralph, *100 Years of Lynching*, Baltimore: Black Classic Press, 1988.
11. O'Reilly, Kenneth, *Racial Matters*, New York: The Free Press, 1989.
12. George, Nelson, *Buppies, B-boys, Baps, and Bohos*, New York: HarperCollins Publishers, Inc., 1992.
13. Bogle, Donald, *Blacks in American Film and Television*, New York: Garland Publications, Inc., 1988.

POST-SEGREGATION BLACK PARENTS: UNWITTING AGENTS OF THE SEDUCTION?

14. Wilson, Amos, *The Developmental Psychology of the Black Child*, New York: Africana Research, 1978.

THE PSYCHOLOGY OF GANGSTERISM: IT EXISTED LONG BEFORE MONSTER KODY SCOTT

15. —,"Hip-Hop's Founding Fathers Speak the Truth," *The Source*, 11/93.
16. Wilson, Amos, *Black-on-Black Violence: The Psychodynamics of Black Self-Annihilation in Service of White Domination*, New York: Afrikan World InfoSystems, 1990.

17. Redding, Saunders, *They Came in Chains: Americans from Africa*, Philadelphia: J.B. Lippincott Company, 1950.
18. McIntyre, Charshee, *Criminalizing a Race: Free Blacks During Slavery*, New York: Kayode Publications, Ltd., 1984.
19. Curry, Leonard P., *The Free Black in Urban America, 1800-1850*, Chicago: The University of Chicago Press, 1883.
20. Marable, Manning, *How Capitalism Underdeveloped Black America: Problems in Race, Political Economy and Society*, Boston: South End Press, 1983.
21. Frederickson, George M., *The Black Image in the White Mind: The Debate on Afro-American Character and Destiny, 1817-1914*, New York: Harper and Row Publishers, 1971.
22. Hutchinson, Earl Ofari, *The Assassination of the Black Image*, Los Angeles: Middle Passage Press, 1994.
23. *Eyes on the Prize: America at the Racial Crossroads 1965-1985*, Boston: Blackside Inc., 1989.
24. O'Reilly, Kenneth, *Racial Matters*, New York: The Free Press, 1989.
25. —,"I Spent Nine Years In Prison For A Crime I Did Not Commit,"*Ebony*, 03/91.
26. "Boston: A Deadly Family Affair," *Newsweek*, 01/15/90.

JUSTICE OR JUSTIFIED OPPRESSION?

27. Bureau of Justice Statistics Sourcebook of Criminal Justice Statistics, 1993.
28. Wall, Brenda, *The Rodney King Rebellion: A Psychopolitical Analysis of Hope and Despair*, Chicago: African American Images, 1993.
29. *"The 'Rodney King' Case: What The Jury Saw in California v. Powell,"* Courtroom Television Network, 1992.
30. Wilson, Amos, *Black-on-Black Violence: The Psychodynamics of Black Self-Annihilation in Service of White Domination*, New York: Afrikan World InfoSystems, 1990.
31. *"Maximum Insecurity,"* Cable News Network, 02/26/95.
32. —,"Discipline by Chiefs is often Overturned," *Dallas Morning News*, 04/21/91.

COUNTERING THE SEDUCTION

33. *"Eyes on the Prize: America at the Racial Crossroads 1965-1985,"* Boston: Blackside Inc., 1989.
34. *"Mission in the Hood,"* Black Entertainment Network, 02/26/95.

35. —,"The New Agenda of The Black Church: Economic Development for Black America," *Black Enterprise*, December 1993.

36. *"Mission in the Hood,"* Black Entertainment Network, 02/26/95.

37. Texas Criminal Laws, *Texas Penal Code*, Austin: 1993-1994.

38. Kunjufu, Jawanza, *Black Economics: Solutions for Economic and Community Empowerment*, Chicago: African American Images, 1991.

39. Kunjufu, Jawanza, *Black Economics: Solutions for Economic and Community Empowerment*, Chicago: African American Images, 1991.

40. —,"Top 50 Black Entertainment Powerbrokers," *Black Enterprise*, December 1994.

BIBLIOGRAPHY

ARTICLES

—,"Bias Begins at Home: A Disturbing Study about Black Self-Image,"*Newsweek*, 08/05/91.

—,"Black-on-Black" Crime: The Myth and the Reality," *Crime and Social Justice*, Issue #20.

—,"Blacks Take Brunt of War on Drugs," *Los Angeles Times*, 04/22/90.

—,"Boston: A Deadly Family Affair," *Newsweek*, 01/15/90.

—,"Combating Gangs in Texas," *Corrections Today*, 07/92.

—,"Discipline by Chiefs is Often Overturned," *Dallas Morning News*, 04/21/91.

—,"Hip-Hop's Founding Fathers Speak the Truth," *The Source*, 11/93.

—,"I Spent Nine Years in Prison for A Crime I Did Not Commit," *Ebony*, 03/91.

—,"More Prisons, More Profit: Black Males Hot Commodity for Corrections Industry," *The Final Call*, 12/20/95.

—,"NAACP Condemns Racist Remarks by Comedian," *Dallas Weekly*, 03/30-04/05/94.

—,"Racial Bias Found in Minnesota's Judicial System," *USA Monitor*, 08/93.

—,"Report Finds Whites Seldom Get Severe Penalties Blacks Get For Selling, Using Crack Cocaine," *Jet*, 06/12/95.

—,"Study Reveals That Most Southern Colleges Remain Segregated," *Jet*, 06/12/95.

—,"Study: News Depicts Blacks in Drug Stories Unfairly," *Jet*, 11/12/90.

—,"Tears of Hate, Tears of Pity," *People Weekly*, 03/13/95.

—,"The New Agenda of the Black Church: Economic Development for Black America," *Black Enterprise*, 12/93.

—,"The Cost of Crime in America," *Business Week*, 12/13/93.

—,"The Myth of Black Violence," *Social Work*, Vol. 38, 07/93.

—,"The Myth of Black Violence," *USA Today* magazine, 01/92.

—,"Top 50 Black Entertainment Powerbrokers," *Black Enterprise*, 12/94.

A USA Today/CNN Gallop Poll on how people perceive the accuracy of television news reports on crime, *USA Today*, 10/28/93.

BOOKS

Akbar, Na'im, *Chains and Images of Psychological Slavery*, Jersey City: New Mind Productions, 1984.

Anderson, Claud, *Black Labor, White Wealth: The Search for Power and Economic Justice*, Edgewood: Duncan & Duncan, Inc. 1994.

Aptheker, Herbert, *American Negro Slave Revolts*, New York: International Publishers, 1970.

Bell, Derrick, *Faces at the Bottom of the Well: The Permanence of Racism*, New York: BasicBooks, 1992.

Bogle, Donald, *Blacks in American Film and Television*, New York: Garland Publications, Inc., 1988.

Browder, Anthony, *From The Browder File: 22 Essays on the African American Experience*, Washington, D.C.: The Institute of Karmic Guidance, 1989.

Brown, Lee, State of Black America 1988, *Crime in the Black Community*, New York: National Urban League, 1988.

Carroll, Charles, *The Negro a Beast or in the Image of God*, St. Louis: The American Book and Bible House, 1900.

Clarke, John Henrik, *Notes for an African World Revolution*, Trenton: African World Press, 1993.

Cose, Ellis, *The Rage of a Privileged Class*, New York: HarperColllins, 1993.

Curry, Leonard P., *The Free Black in Urban America, 1800-1850.*, Chicago: The University of Chicago Press, 1883.

Dubois, W.E.B., *The Souls of Black Folk*, New York: Avon, 1964.

Edelman, Marian Wright, State of Black America Report 1989, *Black Children in America*, New York: National Urban League, Inc. 1989.

Frankel, Marvin, *Criminal Sentences*, New York: Hill and Wang, 1973.

Fraser, George, *Success Runs in Our Race: The Complete Guide to Effective Networking in the African American Community*, New York: Morrow, 1994.

Frederickson, George M., *The Black Image in the White Mind: The Debate on Afro-American Character and Destiny, 1817-1914*, New York: Harper and Row Publishers, 1971.

George, Nelson, *Buppies, B-boys, Baps, and Bohos*, New York: HarperCollins Publishers, Inc., 1992.

Ginzburg, Ralph, *100 Years of Lynching*, Baltimore: Black Classic Press, 1988.

Hacker, Andrew, *Two Nations: Black and White, Separate, Hostile, Unequal*, New York: Maxwell Macmillan International, 1992.

Hare, Nathan; Hare, Julia, *The Miseducation of the Black Child*, San Francisco: The Black Think Tank, 1991.

Hutchinson, Earl Ofari, *The Assassination of the Black Image*, Los Angeles: Middle Passage Press, 1994.

Hutchinson, Earl Ofari, *The Mugging of Black America*, Chicago: African American Images, 1990.

133

Keys, David M., *The Creation and Re-creation of Music: A New Approach to Music Fundamentals*, Englewood Cliffs: Prentice-Hall, Inc., 1995.

Kitwana, Bakari, *The Rap on Gangsta Rap*, Chicago: Third World Press, 1994.

Kunjufu, Jawanza, *Black Economics: Solutions for Economic and Community Empowerment*, Chicago: African American Images, 1991.

Kunjufu, Jawanza, *Hip-Hop vs. Maat: A Psycho/Social Analysis of Values*, Chicago: African American Images, 1993.

Kunjufu, Jawanza, *Lessons from History: A Celebration in Blackness*, Chicago: African American Images, 1987.

Levin, Jack; McDevitt, Jack, *Hate Crimes: The Rising Tide of Bloodshed and Bigotry*, New York: Plenum Press, 1993.

Low, W.; Clift, Virgil, *The Encyclopedia of Black America*, New York: De Capo Press, Inc., 1981.

Marable, Manning, *How Capitalism Underdeveloped Black America: Problems in Race, Political Economy and Society*, Boston: South End Press, 1983.

Martin, Lee, *Unreliable Sources: A Guide to Detecting Bias in Media*, New York: Carol Publishing Group, 1990.

McIntyre, Charshee, *Criminalizing a Race: Free Blacks During Slavery*, New York: Kayode Publications, Ltd., 1984.

Mellon, James, *Bullwhip Days: The Slaves Remember*, New York: Avon Books, 1988.

Murray, Charles; Herrnstein, Richard, *The Bell Curve: Intelligence and Class Structure in American Life*, New York: Free Press, 1994.

Newton, Michael, *Hunting Humans: An Encyclopedia of Modern Serial Killers*, Port Townsend: Loompanies Unlimited, 1990.

O'Reilly, Kenneth, *Racial Matters*, New York: The Free Press, 1989.

Redding, Saunders, *They Came in Chains: Americans from Africa*, Philadelphia: J.B. Lippincott Company, 1950.

Roberson, Erriel, *The Maafa & Beyond: Remembrance, Ancestral Connections and Nation Building for the African Global Community*, Columbia: Kujichagulia Press, 1995.

Rogers, J.A., *The Ku Klux Spirit*, Baltimore: Black Classic Press, 1980.

Russell, Kathy, Wilson, Midge and Hall, Ronald, *The Color Complex: The Politics of Skin Color Among African Americans*, Orlando: Harcourt Brace Jovanovich, Publishers, 1992.

Sitkoff, Havard, *A New Deal for Blacks*, New York: Oxford University Press, 1978.

Swinton, David, State of Black America Report 1989, *Economic Status of Black America*, New York: National Urban League, Inc. 1989.

Trojanowicz, Robert; Bucqueroux, Bonnie, *Community Policing: A Contemporary Perspective*, Cincinnati: Anderson Publishing Company, 1990.

Wall, Brenda, *The Rodney King Rebellion: A Psychopolitical Analysis of Racial Despair and Hope*, Chicago: African American Images, 1992.

Wilson, Amos, *Awakening the Natural Genius in Black Children*, New York: Afrikan InfoSystems, 1992.

Wilson, Amos, *Black-on-Black Violence: The Psychodynamics of Black Self-Annihilation in Service of White Domination*, New York: Afrikan World InfoSystems, 1990.

Wilson, Amos, *The Developmental Psychology of the Black Child*, New York: Africana Research Publications, 1978.

Wright, Bruce, *Black Robes, White Justice*, New York: Carol Publishing Group, 1987.

GOVERNMENT PUBLICATIONS

Black Victims, Bureau of Justice Statistics, 1990.

Criminal Victimization, Bureau of Justice Statistics, 1992.

Deadly Force, National Institute of Justice.

Good for Business: Making Full Use of the Nation's Human Capital, The Federal Glass Ceiling Commission, 1995.

Jail Inmates, Bureau of Justice Statistics, 1990.

National Institute on Drug Abuse, *National Household Survey on Drug Abuse:Population Estimates, 1991*.

Prisoners, Bureau of Justice Statistics, 1990.

Recidivism of Young Parolees, Bureau of Justice Statistics, 1987.

Survey of State Prison Inmates, Bureau of Justice Statistics, 1991.

Texas Criminal Laws, *Texas Penal Code*, Austin: 1993-1994.

The Statistical Abstract of the United States, *Table 644*, Government Printing Office, 1993.

The Statistical Abstract of the United States, *Section 5*, Government Printing Office, 1994.

Uniform Crime Reports 1988, Crime in the United States, Federal Bureau of Investigation, 1988.

Uniform Crime Reports 1993, Crime in the United States, Federal Bureau of Investigation, 1993.

Young Black Americans and the Criminal Justice System: Five Years Later, Bureau of Justice Statistics, 1995.

Young Black Male Victims, Bureau of Justice Statistics, 1994.

STUDIES

"*Eyes on the Prize: America at the Racial Crossroads 1965-1985*," Boston: Blackside Inc., 1989.

"*Innocence and the Death Penalty: Assessing the Danger of Mistaken Executions*," Subcommittee on Civil and Constitutional Rights of the

Committee on the Judiciary, 1993.

"Maximum Insecurity," Cable News Network, 2/26/95.

"Mission in the Hood," Black Entertainment Network, 2/26/95.

"Monitoring the Future," The University of Michigan Institute for Social Research, 1994.

"Muted Voices," National Association of Black Journalists.

"Pathways to Freedom: Winning the Fight Against Tobacco," Fox Chase Cancer Center & The Centers for Disease Control and Prevention, 1992.

"Pelican Bay: California's High-Tech Maximum Security Prison Accused of Torture, Mental Abuse," CBS 60 Minutes, 09/12/93.

"Psychological Screening as it Relates to Police Misconduct," Willingham, Janice, 1991.

"Study in Arrest and Sentencing Dynamics by Race," State of Texas Criminal Justice Policy Council, 02/94.

"The Attempt to Expand Police Powers," ABC Nightline, 02/15/95.

"The 'Rodney King' Case: What the Jury Saw in California v. Powell," Courtroom Television Network, 1992.

"True Colors," ABC Primetime Live, 11/26/92.

Index

Affirmative action, 29
Africa and Africans. See also
    Slavery
    European invasion of, 33-
        34, 53
    free Africans, 39, 73-76
    slavery and, 24-25, 33, 36-
        42, 53, 64-65
    United States relations
        and, 44-45
African Americans. See also
    headings beginning with
    Black
    affluent, 127-128
    as consumers, 117
    as crime victims, 3, 4
    double consciousness of,
        55-56, 122
    income of, 15
    middle class, 60-61, 85
    myths about, 2, 6-8, 16, 18,
        45, 121
    pathway of self-abuse and,
        36
    self-degradation of, 14, 33-
        34, 40, 66-67
    self-hatred of, 2, 27, 43, 52
    split culture of, 53-56
American Colonization
    Society (ACS), 74
American social system, 21-
    22, 34-35, 36, 45, 46
Arrests, 8-12, 87, 90
Assimilation, 58

Bennett, William, 21-22, 82-83
Black communities
Black-on-Black crime and
    violence and, 14-17,61,
    118
    crime in, 1, 87-88, 90
    integration and, 60-61, 110
    legal system collaboration,
        118-120
    perceptions of, 1, 2
    policing in, 10, 89, 101,
        102-118

problem solving and, 106,
    117-118
urban, 58, 60-61
Black crime
    arrests and, 8-12
    causes of, 34-35, 107-128
    genetic predisposition
        myth, 5, 7-8, 18, 28, 35,
        77, 87
    historical role of, 22-24
    labeling of, 5-6
    mass media reporting of, 6-
        8, 12-13, 18-19, 28, 64,
        121, 126
    myths about, 1, 2, 7-8, 13-
        17, 121, 126
    neutralization of, 119, 123
    oppression and, 33, 87-88
    racism and, 30-32
    White control and, 30
    White hysteria over, 23
Black criminalization
    Bennett case and, 83
    Black leadership and, 120
    emancipation and, 76-77
    high-profile Blacks and, 83
    institutional
        criminalization, 86-87
    mass media and, 8, 90,
        124
Black English, 112
Black images
    mass media and, 22, 45,
        77-78, 87, 105
    motion pictures and, 47-49,
        124
    oppression and, 24
    pseudo-science and, 5, 7-8,
        18, 28, 35, 77, 87, 105
Black leadership. See also
    Politics
    African groups and, 44-45
    COINTELPRO and, 80
    development of, 51
    music and, 121, 124-125
    police and, 44, 79
    role of, 120-121
    White domination and, 79

137

Index

Black males
  criminal justice system
    and, 31-32, 95-96, 97
  education and, 112
  images of, 24, 77-78
  race traits of, 8
  redefinition of, 114
Black-on-Black crime and
  violence
  Black communities and,
    14-17, 61, 118
  Black crime labeling and,
    5-6
  Black crime myths and, 2
  Black self-hatred and, 27,
    43
  COINTELPRO and, 44
  oppression and, 6, 36
  police attitudes towards,
    101
  racism and, 5, 66
  statistics regarding, 2-4
Black protest, 78-80
Black social institutions, 51-
  52, 58
Blaxploitation Era, 47, 124
Brown, Joyce Ann, 81-82, 83
Brown v. Board of Education,
  110
Business
  Black middle class and, 60-
    61
  development of, 16, 112,
    114, 117, 127
  religious community and,
    114
Busing, 110

California v. Powell, 86
Carmichael, Stokely, 79-80
Catholic Church, 24-25, 26
Children. See also Family;
  Parents; Youth
  genetic predisposition
    myth and, 18
  optimal child development,
    109-113

  rites of passage for, 115-
    116
  skin color and, 56-57
  teenage Black parents and,
    60
  television and, 46-47
Churches, 52-53, 113-116
Civil rights
  affluent Black Americans
    and, 127
  Black communities as
    watch-dog for, 118
  Civil Rights Movement,
    43, 79
  priority as issue, 6
COINTELPRO (Counter
  Intelligence Program), 44,
  80
Colonizationist Movement, 74
Color-blindness, 106, 117
Columbus, Christopher, 64
Constitutional rights violations, 15-16, 18, 22, 87,
  119
Convict-leasing, 76-77, 96
Counter Intelligence Program
  (COINTELPRO), 44, 80
Crime. See also Black crime
  American perceptions of,
    12-13, 17, 88
  in Black communities, 1,
    87-88, 90
  costs of, 17-19
  as domestic concern, 2
  hate crime, 27-28
  mass media coverage of,
    64, 88, 90
  polls concerning, 1-2, 12-
    13
  prevention of, 97
  prison system effects on,
    94-95
  property crimes, 43
  statistics on, 2-5, 96
  undetected, 11-12
  victims of, 3-4
  white-collar crime, 11, 17,
    93-94

Index

Index

Family. See also Children;
   Parents
   Black middle class and, 60
   integration and, 58
   Maafa and, 53
   skin color and, 56-57
   slavery and, 53
   white domination and, 52-
   53
Farrakhan, Louis, 114
Federal Bureau of Investiga-
   tion, 44, 79-80
Federal Violence Initiative, 18
Free Africans, 39, 73-76

Gangsta rap, 49, 67-71
Gangsterism
gangsta rap and, 67-69
genesis of, 64-66
   internalization of racism
   and, 66-67
   music and, 69-71
   Sanyika and, 63-64
Garvey, Marcus, 44
Ghetto dramas, 48, 124
Glass Ceiling Commission,
   106

Hate crimes, 27-28

Identification principle, 35-36
Imani (faith in God), 109
Individualism, 71, 109, 117
Inferiorization, 46
Institutional criminalization,
   86-87
Integration
   Black communities and,
   60-61, 110
   economics and, 80
   education and, 61, 109-110
   effects of, 58, 110
   legal system and, 80-83
   youth and, 57
Intraracial crime and violence.
   See Black-on-Black crime
   and violence

Jim Crow/legal segregation
   collapse of, 2, 28
   education and, 106-107
   legality of, 26, 77
   racism and, 28
   as social control, 26, 45
   violence and, 42-43
Juvenile justice, 18

King, Martin Luther, Jr., 79,
   79-80
King, Rodney, 86, 118
Ku Klux Klan, 42-43
Kujichagulia (self-determina-
   tion), 109
Kuumba (creativity), 109
Kwanzaa principles, 109

Law enforcement. See Police
Legal system. See also
   Criminal justice system
   Black community collabo-
   ration with, 118-120
   Black protest and, 78-80
   integration and, 80-83
   justice abuse, 74-78
   slavery and, 73
Liberation Theology, 113
Lynching, 36, 42-43, 78

Maafa
   denial of, 33
   destructive effects of, 14
   family support and, 53
   resolving pain of, 107-109
Marcus Garvey School, 112
Mass media
   Black crime coverage, 6-8,
   12-13, 18-19, 28, 64, 126-
   127
   Black crime's historical
   role and, 22-24
   Black criminalization and,
   8, 90, 124
   Black images and, 22, 45,
   77-78, 87, 105, 121

140

Index

Index

affluent Black Americans
and, 127
Black crime myths and, 16
criminal justice system
and, 10-11
police and, 26, 101-102
of status quo, 26-30
Polls, on crime and violence,
1-2, 12-13
Post-traumatic counseling, 36
Prison system
Black males and, 78
Black representation in, 77,
88
convict-leasing and, 76, 77
crime perpetuation and, 94-
95
free Africans and, 74-76
prison ministries, 114
privatization of, 95-97
rehabilitation and, 27
of slavery, 75
statistics on, 12, 91-93
Property crimes, 43
Psychic violence, 36, 39-42,
45-49

Race-neutrality, 106,117
Racial myths. See also Black
images
Black crime and, 7-13
Black-on-Black crime and
violence and, 14-17
definition of, 6-8
genetic predisposition
myth, 5, 7-8, 18, 28, 35,
77, 87
Racism
Black crime and, 30-32
criminal justice and, 80-81
definition of, 29-30
and economics, 9, 10, 12,
14-15
effects of, 5, 52, 108, 127-
128
emancipation and, 76
gangsterism and, 65-67
institutional, 26-27, 33

internalization of, 43, 66-
67, 101
Jim Crow/legal segregation
and, 28
perpetuation of, 26-28
police and, 97, 100-101,
103
prison system and, 91-92,
95
studies of, 29
White domination and, 29-
32
Rehabilitation, 27, 94-95, 97
Religious community, 52-53,
113-116
Rites of passage, 115-116
Ruling elite, 6, 27, 51, 105.
See also White dominance

Segregation. See Jim Crow/
legal segregation
Self-abuse, pathway of, 36
Shakur, Sanyika, 63-64
Simpson, O. J., 23, 97, 100
Skin color
color-blindness and, 106,
117
double consciousness and,
56
family relations and, 56-57
slavery and, 40-42
Slavery
Africans and, 24-25, 33,
36-42, 53, 64
economics and, 73
emancipation from, 76-77
history of, 37-38
legal system and, 73
post-slavery violence and,
42-43
prison system of, 75
resistance to, 25, 38, 54
skin color and, 40-42
trans-Atlantic slave trade
violence and, 36-37
violence and, 37-39
White attitudes towards, 26

142

Index

White domination and, 24-25, 26

Smith, Susan, 22

Social services
  affluent Black Americans and, 127
  white domination of, 16, 106, 107

Southern Christian Leadership Conference (SCLC), 79

Southern Education Foundation, 106

Split culture, 53-56

Sports, 106, 112, 125-126

Stuart, Charles, 21-22, 82-83

Student Non-violent Coordinating Committee (SNCC), 79

Suicide, 43, 66

Supreme Court Racial Bias Task Force, 92

Teenage Black parents, 58-60, 113

Television, 46-47, 88, 123-124

Ten Point Coalition, 113

Ujamaa (cooperative economics), 109, 117

Ujima (collective work and responsibility), 109, 117

Umoja (unity), 109

Undetected crimes, 11-12

United States
  African relations and, 44-45
  crime statistics of, 2-5, 96
  culture of violence, 36
  perception of crime, 12-13, 17, 88
  segregated era of, 2

United States Sentencing Commission, 93

Violence
  Black crime myths and, 16

crime convictions and, 90

Federal Violence Initiative, 18

global African relations and, 44-45

mass media and, 36

material deprivation and, 39

police and, 44

polls concerning, 1-2, 13

post-slavery violence, 42-43

psychic, 36, 39-42, 45-49

slavery phase of, 37-39

trans-Atlantic slave trade phase of, 36-37

Whites and, 36, 78

youth and, 57

Voter registration, 79-80

Weapons, 10, 70

White-collar crime, 11, 17, 93-94

White domination
  of agriculture, 76-77
  American social system control and, 21-22
  Black dysfunctionality and, 24-25
  Black leadership and, 79
  denial of, 26-30
  drug abuse and, 13
  of economics, 34, 51, 105
  family and, 52-53
  mass media and, 22-24
  nationalism and, 26
  oppression and, 25-26, 31-32
  politics of status quo and, 26-30
  racism and, 29-32
  reality of, 5
  in segregated America, 2
  of social services, 16, 106, 107
  voter registration and, 79-80

143

Index